Titian (Ticiano Vecellio, c. 1488-1576)
*Venus and Cupid with a lute player* (c. 1565)
(Fitzwilliam Museum, Cambridge)

# Swarthmore Lecture 1978

# SIGNS OF LIFE:

## art and religious experience

Grau, teurer Freund, ist alle Theorie
Und grün des Lebens goldner Baum
      Goethe: *Faust, Part 1.*
(Gray, cherished friend, is every theory,
And green the golden tree of life.)

FRIENDS HOME SERVICE COMMITTEE · LONDON

First published August 1978

F 54

© John Ormerod Greenwood 1978

ISBN 0 85245 131 8


*Cover design by John Blamires*
The photograph of Komita, the aboriginal artist, on the front cover, is from *Australian Aboriginal Portraits* by Charles P. Mountford.


*Printed in Great Britain in 10/12 Times by Headley Brothers Ltd., 109 Kingsway London WC2B 6PX, and Ashford, Kent*

# PREFACE

The Swarthmore Lectureship was established
by the Woodbrooke Extension Committee at a
meeting held December 9th, 1907 : the minute
of the Committee providing for 'an annual
lecture on some subject relating to the message
and work of the Society of Friends'. The name
Swarthmore was chosen in memory of the
home of Margaret Fox, which was always open
to the earnest seeker after Truth, and from
which loving words of sympathy and
substantial material help were sent to fellow
workers.

The lectureship has a twofold purpose : first, to
interpret further to the members of the Society
of Friends their message and mission ; and,
secondly, to bring before the public the spirit,
the aims and fundamental principles of Friends.
The lecturer alone is responsible for any
opinions expressed.

The lectureship provides both for the publication
of a book and for the delivery of a lecture, the
latter usually at the time of assembly of London
Yearly Meeting of the Society of Friends. A lecture
related to the present book was delivered in the
Great Hall, University of Lancaster, on the evening
of August 13th, 1978.

# FOREWORD

I have kept the briefing which I received from the Swarthmore Lecture Committee before me while preparing this lecture; and (although it may be unusual) I should like to quote it here so that the reader may see what I was asked to do and judge the degree of my success or failure:

> We agree to invite Ormerod Greenwood to give the 1978 lecture on the way in which God can be discovered in and through the arts. In his approach we hope that Ormerod Greenwood will feel able to draw widely on his particular experience of literature and drama, and relate this to Quaker thought and experience. We would also hope that he would feel free to urge upon the Society a wider use of these modes of experience if he considered such a course a suitable development for Quaker life.

I should like to acknowledge the help I have had from members of the Committee who read and commented on the first draft, and of several friends whom I forbear to name although I hope they will be sensible of my appreciation of their criticism and particular assistance.

The cover picture of the Australian artist Komita is reproduced from *Australian Aboriginal Portraits* by Charles P. Mountford (1967), by courtesy of the Melbourne University Press; and the photograph of Titian's *Venus and Cupid with a lute player* by courtesy of the Fitzwilliam Museum, Cambridge. This version of the theme, which Titian painted several times, is thought to date from about 1565, roughly ten years before the painter's death; he was then in his late seventies. The translation of J. L. Borges' poem, *La Moneda de Hierro* (The Iron Coin) is quoted by permission of the editor of *The Times Literary Supplement*, in which it appeared on 6 August 1976.

*John Ormerod Greenwood*

# CONTENTS

# 1

One of my friends telephoned me and asked, in the course of conversation, what I was up to at the moment? 'I am writing a lecture,' I told him, 'on Quakerism and the arts'. 'On Quakerism and the arts!' he said; 'but Quakerism has nothing whatever to do with the arts'. That is indeed the matter at issue, as far as I am concerned; and I thought I had better mention it at the outset, since whatever other persons may think, many of my Quaker capital F Friends don't think it is the matter at all. Everyone concedes that in the early days Quakers were not supposed to go to plays or read novels, or to have anything to do with music or painting, either passively by sitting for their portraits or attending concerts, or actively by owning instruments and performing music, or learning to paint. But in these things, as in many other matters (my Quaker Friends will assure my non-Quaker friend) we have left dead tradition behind us—Quakers may now dance and sing and play the piano, the harpsichord, the crumhorn, the saxophone or the electric guitar to their hearts' content. Even if recitals of classical music at Yearly Meeting are 'unofficial', and 'pop' music—late at night—even more so: still, they have been heard, and no one is going to be disowned for attending. Someone will begin to reel off a list of contemporary Quaker poets for me—Laurence Lerner, Susanne Knowles, Clive Sansom . . . someone else will lead me away to look at the sculpture of Peter Peri, John Spielman or Edward Njenga of Nairobi, or to admire etchings by Robin Tanner; I shall be taken into York Minster to hear the choirs of Quaker schools sing Verdi; or even set down in one of the inspiring gatherings of the Quaker Fellowship of the Arts. Yes, these are signs of life, and we give thanks for them. But it is not a straightforward profit and loss account. On the one hand, the traditional split

1

between Quakerism and the arts—so much more emphatic and complete than in any other Christian body—cannot be obliterated so easily. I know too much, as a historian, about the past of our Society, to be able to disguise the rift; and I have felt too much, in my experience as an artist, to be unconscious of it. If we are to learn anything of 'how God can be discovered through the arts' we must first understand the nature of that rift; and if I am to be any help in the matter, I must uncover something of my own experience.

But I am also conscious of a paradox; on the evidence we have, it seems to me that *in some ways*, in spite of their asceticism, our ancestors were closer to the artistic *experience* than we are: that is, to the beauty and mystery revealed by the imagination. They built finer meeting-houses. They managed to wear very becoming clothes, both the official dress of 'plain Friends' and (when out of 'uniform', as even concerned Friends often were) the handsome costumes of 'the World'. Some practised calligraphy with almost oriental skill and sensitivity; and many found good excuses for practising drawing. They made gardens that sang triumphantly to the Lord. The Gurneys and Frys were not the only ones who loved the culinary arts, even to excess. And beyond dispute, our ancestors wrote better English. You should have spent a few years, as some of us did, winnowing through official documents for inspiring statements to include in the revised version of our Book of Discipline—or even look at those which got through the net. I remember John Hogan reviewing that Book, and saying that everything seemed to stop working after Hannah Kilham, about 1830.

So what did our ancestors have, then, if they weren't supposed to have anything to do with the arts—with music, painting, fiction or the theatre? Well, they had the Scriptures. If you say that we have them too, then you don't know what I'm on about—and half the anguish of writing this lecture has been to try and find a language in which we can understand each other. They were saved from being chained to the letter by the life-giving proviso which Fox and Barclay put so well, declaring that the Scriptures were to be considered as *words* of God, but not as *The Word of God*;[1] and they were provided with a set of landscapes through which the spirit could move, not only through the highest and most noble of human emotions and experiences, but also through the lowest; for as William Blake put it, 'Is not every Vice possible to Man described in the Bible openly?'[2] The Bible was not only read and studied, but lived with from day to day so that any reference, direct or oblique, was caught; each story, anecdote and phrase in the Holy Book was ploughed and sown and reaped again.

The intensity of this experience, derived from a spiritual anthology written in two languages with different backgrounds, and in many styles of verse and prose, is no longer accessible to us. The Bible was translated by great masters under King James, working from older versions which were already slightly archaic at the time, and grew more so as the ages past—but never until now inaccessible. Of course we can still read and love the Scriptures, but we have lost the frame of reference. I mean that there were things which very learned people shared with very simple people, in which the most learned could claim no advantage nor even expect to, because the books they were reading said that the most important things would be shown to the simple and hidden from the wise. Everyone who knew and used this collection of books was like a master composing a vast symphony with hundreds of themes—to touch a note or two was to call up whole patterns. Just take one example, a verse from Psalm 85:

> Mercy and truth are met together;
> Righteousness and peace have kissed each other.

3

Just say it—and how lovely it is to say—and up they come, the Four Daughters of God, who in medieval plays or paintings argue over man's salvation before the throne of God the Father —four beautiful young women, Mercy, Truth, Justice and Peace, each in her robe of appropriate colour and symbolism, pursuing the reconciliation of Divine Justice and Divine Compassion in their (to us) incomprehensible opposition and variety. I have to explain this to you now, and indeed to myself; but there was a time when all I would have needed to say was a few words—'the kiss of Righteousness and Peace' for example —and we should all have been there together, in a shower of variations, developments, improvisations and grace notes. The nearest I have come to it lately has been at the National Theatre's production of the medieval Chester Passion Plays, using the old words but playing them in our own fashion and with our own kind of folk music, with a piece of blue cloth for the river Jordan, and John coming down three steps to baptise the Lord. It is only obliquely that we shall be able to work our way round to something of that experience.

So what happened to the Scriptures? At the end of the nineteenth century we espoused the 'higher criticism' as they called it at the time; and entered with enthusiasm into the detective story which unravelled the various documents which made up *Genesis*, and the relationships of the Synoptic Gospels, and separated the first *Isaiah* from the second, and set *Ecclesiastes* in its Alexandrian context. Well, it was an exciting game, and scientific too, and we learnt a lot. But we knew much less, because the books of the Bible, thrust back into their historic context, were no longer contemporary: Peter had taken off his old sweater and jeans and put on a djibbah or some outlandish garment; and Abraham was a man from an epoch unimaginable years ago whom Leonard Woolley dug up (or did he?) in Ur of the Chaldees. We studied them as creatures from remote cultures, with remote ideas about God or the Gods and the universe; we no longer lived with them like the man next door. Charles Wesley knew what it was to wrestle all night with the Lord, like Jacob:

> Come, O thou Traveller unknown,
>   Whom still I hold, but cannot see,
> My company before is gone,
>   And I am left alone with Thee;
> With Thee all night I mean to stay
> And wrestle till the break of day.

But we were cleverer; we knew about river spirits (thinking of Achilles wrestling with the river Scamander whom the Greeks had polluted with corpses); and about how jealous local Gods were over the invasion of their territories; and we knew about taboos, and how this story was used to explain why the Jews wouldn't eat a certain part of a beast; and with each discovery the experience of wrestling with the unknown God got further and further away. We were liberated from 'Fundamentalism', and it was a genuine liberation: but liberation always exacts a price. The price was exile from the world of myth. As exiles will, we've been busy making our own substitutes—Sherlock Holmes, science fiction, Batman and Star Wars. I'll come back to all that.

To the stories of the Bible, which we shared with the whole of Christendom, our ancestors added their own repertory of Quaker miracles—not that they used that august word: they spoke of 'leadings', 'providences' and 'evidences'. When Thomas Waring, the Quaker stay-maker of Hereford (as William Howitt tells us in his *Year-Book of the Country*)[3] could not sleep on one cold, windy night in winter, he had to rise and mount his horse and ride to Ross-on-Wye, though he could not tell the reason. As he passed over the bridge and entered the town the tall houses were already dark; but he

5

could see a light in one attic window, and knew that his mission lay there. He rode up to the house and knocked; no one came. A boy was passing in the street, and Thomas Waring gave him charge of the horse with instructions to take it to George Dew's, with a message that he would sleep there that night. Thomas waited a long time at the door, until at last a young woman came down and opened it, and timidly asked him his business. He told her in all simplicity that he did not know, but that if she would listen she herself could perhaps explain it. She asked him in, and when she had heard his story she began to weep. She was alone in the house, and she had gone to the attic to put an end to her life. 'Sir,' said she, 'I can tell you why you are come: it is to save me. God has sent you! I am not altogether forsaken or abandoned by him!' Thomas was crying too; 'Thou art not,' he said.

The Quaker repertoire consisted of thousands of such stories, some naive, some elaborately circumstantial; they were told in the family and in meeting, and carried about by visiting ministers, and recorded in commonplace books and printed collections. Surely we need not attempt to prove whether Thomas Waring ever rode to Ross-on-Wye or whether he saved a girl there from suicide? Perhaps there is always a maid in despair in Ross-on-Wye or an *au pair* girl in Sunbury-on-Thames, if there is a Thomas Waring ready to train and then trust his instinct, to ignore ridicule and to live by counsels beyond those of prudence, instead of in 'that great blindness where each is for himself'. Well, it's more exciting than sitting there making stays for fat women, any way. It kept open, for the 'sober' Quakers, the way of spontaneity and adventure as they followed the 'leadings'—the signs of life.

Besides their stories of divine leading, Friends fed their imagination with dreams and visions. If your knowledge of eighteenth-century Quakerism is limited—as it may well be—

6

to the Journal of John Woolman, you may think it a personal eccentricity that he should record with such care and in such detail (and in such beautiful prose) his dreams of 'The Sun Worm', 'The Three Streams in the Green Plain', and the later, unbearably touching dream 'In a time of sickness with the pleurisy'. But this was no personal whim; all Friends were supposed to note, set down and attend to the 'inner promptings' that came from the world of dreams. Notable dreams were copied, along with other 'evidences' and much sadly pedestrian pious verse, into manuscript books, many of which can now be found in the Quaker and other libraries of Britain and America. By their instinctive anticipation of Jung and Freud, the paths between unconscious and conscious were kept open among the Friends, and their imagination survived even the isolation in which they had placed it when they renounced the arts. We have to ask why we, who are in name so much more free, seem less endowed than they. The fierce psychic drives within them found an outlet and a release.

The ministers of that time had a startling phrase for the validation of their 'openings': *I saw it in that which does not lie*. What a wonderful, daring claim! The only field of vision where I would ever expect to find it made today would be in the arts: *I saw it in that which does not lie*. Once a work has that quality it will not fade, whether it was made thirty thousand years ago or yesterday: its age, background, language, symbols are immaterial; it is permanent.

For us, in theory, the canon of scripture is never closed.[4] We could have made more of that precious truth. 'A masterpiece is part of the conscience of mankind.'

## 2

The earliest identifiable human activity, apart from eating, sleeping and sex, hunting and gathering, is the practice of art.

Before men tilled the ground or lived in cities or invented the wheel, they painted with skill, precision and truth. The cave paintings of Europe, dating back 25,000 years or more, generally represent the great beasts which men hunted and cherished; but among them, in a cave of the Auvergne, stands man identifying with them, man as performer. There he stands in the darkness of the centuries, covered in a beast's pelt, antlered and masked and tailed but with touchingly human feet and toes peeping out: man as stag. Whatever he was doing in that lost ritual of unimaginable years ago, be sure that what he sought was unity with the creation by becoming what he was not. A lonely ritual: he stands by himself in the darkness, unattended, and perhaps the incredible courage *that* demanded was part of the spell; but the ritual was for the benefit of all. Though remote from us, it is perhaps not so remote as we think; once a year in the Staffordshire village of Abbot's Bromley they still perform the Horn Dance with reindeer horns (reindeer?—in Abbot's Bromley?) And on every stage the world around, from the classical theatre of Japan to the latest American musical, from the Nigerian village to the English village hall, the actor still does what he always did: he assumes a character which is not his own, and he is only able to do so because we are all one. Otherwise how could he make the leap from one skin to another, from one face to another, from one heart to another; or make those of us who are watching aware of what he is doing?

I have mentioned four continents—let us make it five. For here is a photograph (on our cover) reproduced from a book published eleven years ago, of the Australian aboriginal artist Komita. Like the artist of 25,000 years ago, he still goes to the caves to make paintings, using red ochre, 'the most expensive material in their culture'. From him you may learn about *kuranita*, that mysterious life essence which permeates the whole of nature, 'whose presence means life, and whose absence death'. Here in our photograph he sits on the sand in the sun; naked, erect, benign, he makes with his finger the art that is magic and the magic that is art: the concentric circles of existence. The wind will blow away his beautiful design as it has blown away Richard Burbage's performance of Hamlet and Ben Jonson's *Masque of Queens*, but the magic has been made and it can be re-made. 'The spring flowers are permanent', said the Indian poet Tagore, 'because they know how to die'. The signs of life are in the renewal of life; the heart of religion is in resurrection. The signs of life are what we look for and hope for, as simple and mysterious as Komita's concentric circles, or the sacred spiral which returns constantly to almost—but never quite—the same place. Australia has been a cruel step-mother to Komita and his kind, who are among the loveliest and least destructive of human beings; but Australia lies deeper and deeper in their debt, for the vision of herself is impregnated by the dream-time.

Art, religion and magic grew up together. There was no such thing, in the beginning (and for Komita and his people there is still no such thing) as dance, or story, or prayer; but there was dance that was music that was story that was incantation that was drama; there was no sculpture, but there was sculpture that was image that was prayer that was healing that was safety that was power that was mask that was revelation: all in one, and one in all. Drama grew out of religion in ancient classical Greece, with the coming of Dionysus; in medieval Japan, Korea, Tibet and China, with the coming of Buddhism; in medieval Europe, with the coming of Christianity. Architecture grew out of religion in the Parthenon, and in the temples of Angkor-Wat, and the Gothic cathedrals and the mosques of Islam. The paintings of Giotto and the music of Bach came out of religion. In India there are temple dancers

9

who dance for the Gods alone; in medieval Europe men carved invisible corners of church roofs for God and the angels; and in a cell in Bedlam Christopher Smart wrote *Rejoice in the Lamb* for no human ear. But nothing is lost, and sometimes we are lent the eyes of God. The television camera shows us the grave beauty of the girl dancing alone in the Temple court-yard; the telephoto lens shows us the invisible beauties of the cathedral roof; and the printing press brings us the text of Kit Smart's poem, so that we too may rejoice in the antics of his cat Jeoffrey, 'for the divine spirit comes about his body to sustain it in complete cat'[5] (just like Komita's divine essence, *kuranita*); and when we have read or seen or listened, we can join in Smart's lunatic hymn of praise:

> For I bless the Lord Jesus from the bottom of Royston
> Cave to the top of King's Chapel.
> For I am a little fellow, which is intitled to the great
> mess by the benevolence of God my father.

In art, nothing is lost, and the past co-exists with the present. The poets before Homer are present in Homer, for they taught him his art and bequeathed him his verse and his themes; and Homer is present in Pope and in Keats. The music of Josquin des Pres is sung again after five hundred years. African masks leap out of museum cases to inspire Picasso; Japanese prints give new eyes to the French Impressionists. Beowulf is set to new music; a fifteenth-century nonsense rhyme becomes the theme of a pop-song;[6] Simon and Garfunkel revive the spells of the magic herbs in *Scarborough Fair*, which can be traced back to the Middle Ages; and the awe-inspiring winter resurrection ritual of the dying year in the traditional English Mummers' Play is taken into the repertoire of the folk-rock group, Steeleye Span. Not that the fans care; to them all this is already ten years old, and so prehistoric—I am talking about 'golden oldies' in their patronising phrase, and Simon and Garfunkel, and Steeleye Span have already broken up. But that doesn't alter the fact; art adds to our concept of hurrying time the dimension of eternity which is part of religion.

Art, magic and religion grew up together, and they should stay that way, though we may owe our sense of their continuity in part to the methods we have found of investigating the past—the printing press, the new media, ways of information storing and retrieval and research and presentation. As the world shrinks and cultures are shaken up and mingled, and Korean violinists perform Mozart and Beethoven, and British pop stars go to India to learn the sitar, and musicologists to Indonesia to study the gamelan, and Benin bronzes take their place among the world's masterpieces, and Shakespeare plays are performed in Tashkent and Peter Brook leads his cosmopolitan company to perform in African townships, and Japanese players bring their fourteenth-century Nō plays to Paris and London, and Anglo-American pop records are played in Malagasy villages . . . we stand almost overwhelmed in our Aladdin's cave of treasures, marvelling at the universality of our inheritance, at man's adaptability and at his power to create; at the openness which enables him to discover and interpret, and the humility and patience which enables him to learn—all those virtues which we forget when we look only at his insane pride, his jealousy, his blind vulgarity and self-centredness.

But if art and religion belong together, how and why did they become separated in Quakerism, except so far as they could be preserved by instinct and innocent subterfuge? And why should we still be troubled by a sense of loss, if the mistakes of tradition are being reversed, and the arts re-admitted to Quaker respectability? We must now perform a dutiful piece of Quaker ritual, most proper for a Swarthmore lecture, and

11

examine the experience of early Friends. It will be a bit of a change to present them unfavourably, instead of marvelling at their heroism, insight and matchless achievements as we are accustomed to do.

## 3

I have paid our ancestors the warmest and most sincere tribute that I know how, having lived with their experience and profited from it for half a century. I am therefore entitled to examine their apostasy, the price which they paid for it and the price which we pay for it, and to ask with tenderness whether we are yet free of the burden which they imposed on us, through what seems to me (and to an increasing number of us) a very grave misreading of the divine purpose.

A familiar and famous episode in our early history concerns Solomon Eccles (or Eagles) who 'went naked for a sign'—though I hasten to add that he was quite as decent as any father of a family on Bournemouth beach, since he wore a sailor's blue neckerchief girt about his private parts. He walked through London with a brazier of burning sulphur on his head, and you will sympathise more easily if you know that the day before, our meeting in Gracechurch Street had been raided, and one man clubbed so severely that he died a few days later. Many people thought Solomon Eccles mad, and many still do, so we'd better take the opinion of our first historian, William Sewel,[7] who knew him:

> Altho' some reckoned him out of his wits, yet he was not, for I remember the Time very well, and had many an Opportunity to see and to hear him speak . . . He was an extraordinary zealous Man, and what he judg'd Evil he warmly opposed, even to the Hazard of his Life . . . he was, to my Knowledge, a bold and undaunted Man.

Clearly George Fox thought the same, or he would not have taken Eccles with him to America in 1671, at a very critical time.

Solomon Eccles was a musician from a family of musicians. He could make instruments, play on them, compose for them; and he got his living by teaching: 'I could teach men's Sons and Daughters on the Virginals and on the Viol, and I got the last two years more than an hundred and thirty pounds a year with my own hands'. If you read his pamphlet, *A Musick-Lector* (1667) you may agree that he was sane enough. It embodies a dialogue between 'three men of several judgments . . . The one a Musician, and Master of that Art, and zealous for the Church of England; who calls Musick the gift of God. The other a Baptist, who did affirm it to be a *decent* and *harmless practice*. The other a Quaker (so called) being formerly of that Art, doth give his Judgment and Sentence against it, but yet approves of the Musick that pleaseth God.'

The 'Musick that pleaseth God' refers, in his view, to the inner music of the spirit; but as for the 'Babylonish Trade of Musick'—he abandoned all that and learned to make clothes and cobble shoes for a living. He sold his 'Instruments of Vanity', his music books and instruments; but then decided they should be destroyed, so he bought them back again and took them 'Virginals, Fiddles and all to Tower-hill where, laying them all together, he set fire to them'. In *A Musick-Lector*[8] he tells us the outcome:

> . . . and when the fire flamed upon them, the rude multitude would not suffer me to burn them, but put the fire out; so I was forced to stamp upon them and break them to pieces; for I did it with much indignation; though my Father and Grandfather, and Great-Grandfather were Musicians, yet He that was before Sin was taught me to do as I did . . . The same indignation is with me still against

this practice, as against Lying, and Stealing, and committing Adultery; yet there is something in Musick, but there is a difference between the Harps of God and the Harps of Men, as there is a difference between the Natural Man and the Spiritual Man.

To measure his sacrifice, turn to the page where he describes what music once meant to him:

I was once playing a part with four more, more than 30 years ago; and the parts hit with the Fuige (Fugue) and came in with the Discords and Concords so very lovely, *that it took very much with that part which stands not in unity with the Lord:* so that a Master of Musick being in the room at the same time, heard the parts, and took his Hat off his Head, and flang it on the ground, and cryed aloud, saying, Now take Body and Soul and all! This he said who never knew what his Soul was, nor what it could cost to redeem it from destruction. So I see that Musick pleases well that which is for destruction, and grieves that which God doth highly esteem and honour.

At one of those moments which occur rarely in a musician's or anyone else's lifetime, when everything is going perfectly and you are lifted out of this world into another dimension and the only thing you can feel is unspeakable content and harmony which you wish might never cease—at this very moment Solomon Eccles tears himself away from the experience of Transfiguration, 'take Body, Soul and all', because he feels that it is 'so very lovely, that it took very much with that part which stands *not* in unity with the Lord'. Music, he thought, belongs among the temptations of this World that seduce us from eternal life.

I feel as vividly for him personally as if I had stood on Tower-hill and heard the crunch of his boot on the wafer-thin belly of his viols—if only I could get him from the grave to tell me why the loveliness of music should *not* be in unity with the Lord. But I also feel terror and disgust at what this incident represented for the Society of Friends—and more widely, for the future of our divided culture. It reinforces my horror, which several key incidents of my personal experience have taught me, of the *certainty* of men of principle; I want to say, as Cromwell did to the Church of Scotland: 'I beseech you, in the bowels of Christ, think it possible you may be mistaken'. For Solomon Eccles's attitude was shared by almost the whole of the Society of Friends, including George Fox; and all the arts were banished, with the whole weight of the Discipline, both from our worship and from the domestic lives of Friends, until the late nineteenth century.

While Solomon Eccles was away with Fox in the West Indies and the new Plantations, his family were able to pursue their musical studies. In the sixteen-eighties, just before old Solomon died, compositions began to appear in the name of his son, also called Solomon. Another son, Henry, became a violinist in the royal band, the 'King's Musick' and then went to Paris to enter the most famous orchestra of the time, 'Les Violons du Roi' of the Sun-King, Louis XIV; and in Paris Henry Eccles edited collections of violin music from Italian originals, some of which is still played. Most famous of the family, however, is Solomon Eccles's grandson, John Eccles; he collaborated with Henry Purcell in *Don Quixote*, composed masques and operas to words by Congreve, Dryden, D'Urfey and Ravenscroft; set the songs and wrote the music for such masterpieces as *Venice Preserv'd*, *Love for Love* and *The Way of the World*; and in 1700 became Master of the King's Musick. He wrote the coronation music for Queen Anne. For twenty years he was the leading composer for the theatre, at a time when the theatre was the chief public place where music could be heard (since concerts were still a novelty). In 1710 he published nearly one hundred of his songs, and if you think that you have never heard any of them—well, if you have heard *The Beggar's Opera*, you have. Now that English baroque music is being studied afresh, John Eccles is becoming an important figure; one recent writer praises 'the freshness and flow of his melodies'; another calls his opera *Semele* 'the one work of the early eighteenth century which might have contributed towards the creation of a national opera';[9] it has recently been revived and broadcast.

So the musical talent of the Eccles family, in spite of old Solomon, persisted through at least seven generations, from his great-grandfather to his grandson; they might legitimately be called one of the most consistently gifted musical families in our history. But now mark the point in the British musical scene—the moment when Purcell lay prematurely dying, and our music, which had held its place with the best since the fifteenth century, suddenly faltered. Italian opera overwhelmed us, and Georg Friedrich Händel had to come from Germany to rescue us. Perhaps John Eccles has been undervalued, as he was certainly unlucky; but suppose for a moment that the Quakers, instead of being at the point of the wedge which split our culture and made us the most Philistine people in Western Europe, had been behind him. Suppose that they had loved, understood, valued, fostered music, and cradled the talent of this abandoned orphan of theirs in sharp and sensitive critical appreciation . . . then we might be talking today about the Eccles family as Germans talk of the family of Bach, who drew strength from, and occasion from, and provocation from their Lutheran background. What we are discussing today is more than a mere parochial matter.

It would be comforting to treat Solomon Eccles's conduct as a personal aberration, or an example of extreme Puritanism;

but that would not be fair. After all, in his dialogue the Anglican calls music 'the gift of God' and the Baptist defends it as 'a decent and harmless practice'; and we know that John Bunyan showed his love of music in *The Pilgrim's Progress*, while Oliver Cromwell not only kept his private musicians, but allowed his political enemy Sir William Davenant to produce the first operas in England, and with women singers too. Puritans were not against music, but among the Quakers, the anathema was spoken, and by no one more emphatically than Fox himself:

> testifying against their Wakes or Feasts, their May-games, Sports, Plays and Shows, which trained up People to Vanity and looseness . . . I was moved to cry also against all sorts of Musick, and against the Mountebanks playing tricks on their Stages, for they burdened the pure Life, and stirred up people's minds to Vanity.[10]

We need not multiply the evidence. There were exceptions, of course; William Penn's wife Gulielma carried her lute across the fields to play to blind John Milton; and knowing Milton, we may be sure she was an accomplished performer. But as principles hardened into rules, the arts of music, drama and painting were excluded from the lives of Friends. It seems to have been the loss of music that hit the hardest. Edwin Alton,[11] in a study of the subject, tells us of David Fox who joined us in 1828, and buried his cello in the garden because he could not rightly play it, sell it or give it away. Neave Brayshaw tells us of a Friend who kept his flute, and once a year took it to the top of the Monument in London for a solitary blow, where it could do least harm; William Jones, secretary of the Peace Society and a leading spirit in the 'War Vics' of 1870, tells us how his father John, the first Friend in the family, had to abandon the triple Welsh harp, which he had spent ten years

in learning, when he joined us.[12] Of course there were sensible
people, like the great scientist John Dalton (who was certainly
a consistent Friend) and who, having failed in a petition to
Yearly Meeting in his youth to be allowed the use of music,
went off to the theatre and to the opera during his scientific
trips on the continent. Elizabeth Fry's husband Joseph used to
steal away to concerts with the children, leaving Elizabeth
longing to join them; and for how many sad souls did Amelia
Opie speak when she wrote in her *Farewell to Music* in 1854:

> Thou shalt rob me no more of sweet silence and rest,
> For I've proved thee a trap, a seducer at best.

And she the wife of a fashionable painter, at that!

By the end of the nineteenth century attitudes had been
relaxed, very gradually: pianos appeared in Quaker homes
without bringing disownment, and Quaker children learnt to
sing and play the cello. But the theatre was still unacceptable,
and Annie Horniman repeated, in terms of the drama, the
Eccles experience in music. With an inheritance from her
father John Horniman (the first man to put tea in packets)
she anonymously backed the first performance of Shaw's
*Arms and the Man* in 1894; went on to provide the Irish
with the Abbey Theatre; launched the repertory movement
in Manchester and produced 200 plays there, many by new
writers. But she could only do this by renouncing her
birthright.

At the epoch-making Manchester Conference of 1895,
when so many controversial matters were brought out and
aired and new life flowed through the Society, I can find only
one extensive reference to the arts.[13] It came from Thomas
Hodgkin, banker and historian and man of culture; and he
admits that in the past we may have been 'too Puritan, almost
Manichean, in our attitude towards Art'. But in the disguise

of penitence, he introduces a new and much more dangerous heresy: the attack on *contemporary* art. 'For human conduct and human happiness,' he still maintains, 'it is far safer to ignore Art altogether, than it is to accept her as the sole guide and arbiter of human life'. His misgivings are ostensibly based on the current doctrine of 'Art for Art's sake'; but his real quarrel is with the influence of art on moral codes, and its claim to bring all human life, ugly as well as beautiful, into its compass:

> Now Art threatens to become Religion in another sense, obliterating all the old landmarks of morality, and deciding by herself, and with reference to artistic considerations alone, what is fitting and becoming in human life.

> 'Everything,' so runs the present doctrine, 'which *is*, is worthy of being copied by the artist. Untruth in art is the one unpardonable sin. If that is avoided, what men have called immoralities, or even crimes, may pass with light censure.' The teaching falls on willing ears. The flesh is only too ready to do its manifest works; and so, under the influence of these new doctrines (derived in great measure from France, but rapidly naturalised in England) painting becomes indecent, fiction filthy, and the drama—so we are told—a school of vice.

What examples could Thomas Hodgkin have been thinking of in 1895? He mentions none; so are we to suppose that he was thinking of the novels of Thomas Hardy, who in that year published the last of them, *Jude the Obscure*, to the usual chorus of obloquy? And in the field of drama, which '*we are told* is a school of vice' was it the banned play *Widowers' Houses* by that terrible Bernard Shaw, or those still more shocking foreigners Henrik Ibsen and August Strindberg whose disgusting sewer dramas were causing riots throughout Europe? And then, those French paintings! In 1895 the French government was offered a bequest of 65 Impressionist pictures by Manet, Monet, Cézanne, Renoir, Sisley, Pissarro and Degas, but officials advised rejection on the ground that 'only moral depravity could bring the State to accept such rubbish'. Which French writers did Thomas Hodgkin find corrupting—was it Verlaine, dreaming of Parsifal:

> En robe d'or il adore, gloire et symbole
> Le vase pur où resplendit le Sang réel,
> — Et ô ces voix d'enfants chantant dans la coupole!
> (In golden robe he worships glory and symbol, the shining vessel of the Holy Grail—and O those children's voices singing in the dome above.)

Or was it Rimbaud, crying in the anguish of his adolescence, before he fell silent for ever:

> Si Dieu m'accordait le calme céleste, aérien, la prière —
> comme les anciens saints — Les saints! des forts! les anachorètes, des artistes comme il n'en faut pas.
> (If only God granted me calm like the great arch of heaven, prayer like the saints of old—what strength they had, the saints, the hermits—artists of a kind now missing from the earth.)

If any of these were the names that Thomas Hodgkin had in mind—and they were the controversial names of 1895—then history has not justified him. The reputation of the French *poètes maudits* and the great Impressionist painters belie him; and Hardy, Shaw and Wilde, not to speak of Ibsen and Strindberg, have become our masters and our teachers. Hodgkin denounces the claim that 'untruth in Art is the one unpardonable sin'. Oh Thomas, doubting Thomas, Quaker

Thomas, untruth *anywhere* is the unpardonable sin; and it is because they spoke truth to us about the human condition—cost what it might—that we do trust the artists, and they *have* changed our values. 'It is the business of art and of letters,' young Willie Yeats was saying at the time, 'to change the values and mint the coinage';[14] and Delacroix (but then, he was French, so we'd better watch him) said that 'It is in using the language of one's contemporaries that one must, as it were, teach them the things that language does not express'.[15] In doing these things, the artists are about their father's business; they are leading us into those other mansions of which Christ spoke; and they pay the price, as he warned them they would, of exile (like Ibsen), imprisonment (like Verlaine and Wilde) poverty (like Verlaine and Shaw) and estrangement (like Hardy). The great success of that summer of 1895 in the theatre was *The Importance of being Earnest* by Oscar Wilde; so successful indeed, that they kept it on when the author went to gaol, with the simple compromise of deleting his name. While Thomas Hodgkin in Manchester was denouncing the code of the aesthetes, Wilde was writing from Reading Gaol: 'The plank bed, the loathsome food, the hard ropes shredded into oakum till one's finger-tips grow dull with pain, the silence, the solitude, the shame,—each and all of these things I have to transform into a spiritual experience. There is not a single degradation of the body which I must not try and make into a spiritualising of the soul.'[16]

When you read these words, you will not think that I am flogging a dead controversy into a pretence of life. You could set them beside those last dying words of James Nayler after a not dissimilar experience of pain and disgrace and isolation from those he loved best: 'I found it alone, being forsaken; I have fellowship therein with them who lived in Dens, and desolate places in the Earth.' They belong together.

21

*4*

But in defending the artists of the nineties against Thomas
Hodgkin's strictures, I have brought back into mind the anxiety
with which I began writing this lecture: the absence of a 'frame
of reference' which we could all share, and without which
anything I have to say might make no sense at all. For how do
I know whether you have ever seen *Widowers' Houses* or
*Little Eyolf* (written in 1894), or whether you have read *Jude
the Obscure* or Verlaine's *Confessions* (1895)? You have
probably seen Impressionist paintings (how could you avoid
it?) but you have certainly not seen them with the eyes of the
French official who called them depraved rubbish; on the
other hand you might be quite ready to apply this phrase to
Picasso's *Les Demoiselles d'Avignon* (1907) or to Paul Klee's
*La Belle Jardinière* (1939) assuming that you have ever seen
them; and they are ancient history by now. So where is there a
common point where we could start together? Why don't we
look at the most expensive and elaborate work of art created
by our Society during the past half-century—I mean Friends
House in Euston Road in London; after all, it won a prize as
'the best building of its year'.

It stands with its classical front and pillared portico opposite
the station. The front doors are normally kept locked, in case
the public might think there was something going on there;
and business is done at the side door, like the farmhouse where
we used to buy milk and eggs. Don't go in yet; let us follow the
advice of Teresa of Avila to her novices—she told them that
she did not expect any great matter from their understandings,
but merely that they should look. Have you noticed anything
about the doors? Over each lintel stands the fasces, the sculp-
tured representation of a bundle of rods bound with a thong.
In ancient Rome, from which this symbol is derived, the fasces
were surrounded by legend and protocol; they went back in

tradition to the days of the ancient Kings, and passed from them to the highest magistrates of the Republic, and then to the Roman Emperors. They were carried over the shoulders of lictors, and must be lowered in the presence of the popular assembly or of higher officials. Dictators were entitled to 24 fasces; consuls and kings to 12; proconsuls 6; imperial legates 5; praetors 2, and vestal virgins 1.

Why have I pillaged the classical dictionaries to tell you all this? To bring out the extraordinary inappropriateness of the symbol to its present use. Suppose that the architect had designed his beautiful large Meeting-house with a gigantic Cross behind the clerks' table, what agitated sessions there would have been in the Meeting for Sufferings, what an avalanche of letters to *The Friend*! Be sure that the fasces of the Roman governor were there when Pilate sentenced Jesus; so we set over our doors, as it were over some Roman court-house, the symbol of the power which destroyed our leader. Why?

The answer, so far as it goes, is fairly straightforward. The fasces adorn Friends House for the same reason that eighteenth-century statesmen on their tombs in Westminster Abbey wear the toga instead of coat and breeches: because of the unfailing pull of ancient Rome. The twentieth century architect wanted to build for us a house of proper *gravitas*, weight and solemnity, and so—like any eighteenth-century gentleman in Somerset or Virginia—he designed it in the most imposing, that is, Roman, style. Naturally he carried into his design details from the copy-books. What a fuss I am making, I shall be told (and have already been told) over a trivial matter, when the world is so full of important themes more appropriate to a Swarthmore lecture!

Unfortunately, the symbol was not quite dead. At the very moment when the masons of Messrs. Grace and Marsh were hoisting our fasces into place over the Friends House portals, Benito Mussolini was parading his through imperial Rome. The murder of the Socialist deputy Matteotti was on 10 June 1924. Mussolini too wanted his movement to have *gravitas*, so he called his men *Fascisti*, bearers of the symbol of power, the men of order (the neat pack of rods) and of unity (the rods bound together for strength); they would give back to Italy its imperial greatness and make the world take notice, through the old Roman sense of discipline. Henceforth, the trains would run to time.

So the symbol retained its power; but if architecture is to have a language at all, its use in Friends House argued an extraordinary illiteracy, shared by the Royal Institute of British Architects, their prize-winning architect, his clients and the public. It is harder to think of a better example of blind tradition, preventing everyone from asking the key question: What should a Quaker Meeting-house be like? If the architect, himself a Quaker, had read the symbol; or if any of his clients on the committee had had the courage to ask, 'What is this funny thing over the door?' would our portals ever have been crowned with the lictor's rods? But in the Roman world, everyone could read the sign: 'Roman justice and power rule here'.

This illiteracy has become a central phenomenon of Western society since the Reformation. We may now, even the most puritanical of us, lament the iconoclasm of that period, the destruction of statues, paintings and stained glass, the wounds which are still apparent in our most beautiful churches. But we have lost not only works of art, we have lost a whole way of thinking, of looking, of reacting, of perceiving and of penetrating the universe of which we are a part. The old order was brought to an end in a fury of release—the fury expressed in Quaker terms by Solomon Eccles's bonfire on Tower-hill.

As the glorious artefacts went clattering down in dust and fragments of stone, wood and glass, there was a sense of liberation. The old chains had gone, the old lies had lost their power; men were set free to seek the Truth. More whole-heartedly than most, the Quakers renounced the old ways of picture-thinking; not merely the idolatry of the rows of saints, the *schema* of salvation depicted in 'God's own house', but the rites of water-baptism and the 'Lord's supper' and the use of the ring in marriage. God needed no such rites; his house was not a 'steeple-house' but the universe, 'the spacious firmament on high' where he had written his immutable laws according to reason and logic. Through reason, the divine key, men set themselves humbly to discover and investigate the laws of the universe; and then to employ them in those inventions which have given us the world of science and technology, in creating which our tiny sect has had so disproportionately rich and distinguished a part. But it is time to say with Friedrich Nietzsche: 'We have Art in order that we may not perish from Truth.'[17]

Now let us go into the house.

## 5

While Friends House was being built, Joseph Southall, a painter who was a member of the Society, fortified himself with the fact that a new edition of *Christian Faith and Practice* admitted the arts to a degree of Quaker respectability, and wrote to *The Friend* to suggest that artists should be allowed to cover the walls of the new building with paintings; for he did not accept Thomas Hodgkin's view that the artist's job is to copy or to represent, and quoted the Book of Discipline in evidence:[18] 'The artist at his best is not a mere imitator or reproducer but a creator . . . He shares the power of the Divine Creator.

25

He reveals new truths, and opens our eyes to wonders we never dreamed of.' Naturally, it did not happen; the walls of Friends House, as you can see for yourself, remain bare.

But across the other side of the world, the group of Chinese Quakers in Szechwan, with that sense of clanship and friendship which never fails the Chinese however scattered the family may be, heard of our new House in London and to wish us well, sent us in a gracious gesture of celebration 'two embroidered scrolls and a vase'. One scroll remains, framed under glass at the head of the stairs on the first floor of Friends House. Let us look at it, still following St Teresa's advice. It might help us to consider what Arnold Schoenberg said to those who found his music difficult: 'Forget the theories, and if possible, the author: "A Chinese poet speaks Chinese, but what is it he says?".'

Our panel depicts episodes from the Hundred-Chapter-Novel by Wu Ch'eng-en, called the Hsi-yu Chi, or *Journey to the West*. The journey it speaks of was an actual journey which took place, in historic terms, between 629 and 645 AD by Hsüan-chuang, who died in 664 AD. He went to India to seek instruction, to learn Sanskrit and to collect Buddhist texts; and his sixteen-year journey has always been counted, with justice, among the great individual exploits of Chinese history. The huge Chinese classical libraries still bear the name which was apparently his title of honour, the Tripitaka. So far, we have been dealing with history; and in sending pictures of this teacher and benefactor, our Chinese Friends seem to have drawn a parallel which implies a compliment. Just as Hsüan-chuang endured danger and privation on his journey, so did our missionaries on their shorter, but almost equally difficult and dangerous journeys to Szechwan to bring fresh light to its people. They went East, from our European point of view, but West to West China (in Chinese terms)—so they too made a Hsi-yu Chi, a *Journey to the West*; and the parallel carries a Quaker moral. There is, to use Robert Barclay's expression, 'a universal saving light'—there were saints and heroes in China before the Christian missionaries, and instead of waiting for light to be brought to them, they took their lives in their hands and went out to find it. The compliment paid by our Chinese Friends implies a deep understanding of Quaker doctrine, but it also carries a warning: do not disparage or underestimate us; you were not the first servants of the Light. And the warning in turn conveys a promise: even in the Gobi desert and among the highest of the snow peaks, Hsüan-chuang found help. Do not despair, there are always friends of the Light.

There were heroes before Agamemnon, as Horace said;[19] but in this case they did not, as Horace lamented, lack a sacred poet. But the 'sacred poet' whose book supplies the episodes depicted on our scroll, Wu Ch'eng-en, lived in the time of Shakespeare, a thousand years after the historic events we have been describing. Like Homer, he drew on centuries of story-telling and drama, developed from the central germ of fact. Our embroidery is no Bayeux tapestry of historic events, it is fabulous. The first versions of the story now extant date from the fourteenth century, about the time of Chaucer in our western time-scale. Episodes were also being used by that time for plays, even for those given by the lowest troupes of travelling players. The story still went on being told and acted in market-places down to the nineteenth century.

Even in his own life-time Hsüang-chuang had become the subject of legend, and in the course of centuries (as with his close historical contemporary King Arthur of Britain) magic and fantasy had taken over. King Arthur had Knights of the Round Table who performed prodigious feats against ogres and dragons; and Tripitaka acquired companions for his journey, helpers and enemies. There was the Stone Monkey, Sun Wu-kung, who perhaps came from the Indian monkey-god Hanumat; and Mr Pig, Chu-pa-chieh, who by a lamentable mistake was the son of a sow and broke the eight commandments, and liked to eat little children. He, and the beautiful White Horse who was once a dragon—reminding us of our own mysterious White Horse cut on the chalk downs, and active in Welsh legend—perhaps came from prehistoric cults of the pig and the horse. You can see the splendid Horse in our embroidery, and watch Mr Pig with his terrifying rake, about to destroy two children tied to a gate. But the villagers implore Kuan-yin, the Goddess of Mercy, who is a benefactor to all of us. She saved Sun, the Monkey, after his outrageous tricks against Heaven, during which he ate the peaches in the celestial garden, the fruit of immortality. He is imprisoned for centuries under rock until he is released to help the Traveller; but his brows are bound with an iron hoop (or crown of thorns, in some versions of the story) which tightens when he gets too outrageous. So at last, as we see in the concluding episode of our own scroll, which of course is read from right to left in Chinese fashion, they all return home to a royal welcome. History, in which the actual pilgrim defied an Imperial edict by travelling to the West, has given place to the different truth of fable. By the time Wu Ch'eng-en made his version, allegory and allusion had become part of the reading of the tale; it had probably begun long before, since an early Buddhist poem teaching self-control says that

> The three ways of discipline exorcise the Horse-of-Desire,
> The six kinds of recollection still the Monkey-of-the-Mind.[20]

It was easy for Monkey, Horse and Pig to become characters of drama, and they can be found in fourteenth-century plays based on Taoist symbols. So when they got to Wu's Hundred-Chapter-Novel they had a rich, complex derivation. Like Shakespearean clowns, who also come down from the magical world of folk-lore, they give extra dimensions to the story; they are funny, touching, frightening, grotesque, amoral, nonsensical by turns: they show us human waywardness, nastiness, folly, greed, slyness—what you will.

The novel from which our picture is derived has often been called 'A Buddhist Pilgrim's Progress' and the label, though trite, is very apt. Bunyan too found his theme in a long tradition of medieval folk-tale, play and poem; and he has his own strange dragon-figure of Apollyon, his Giant Despair, and his Faithful Friend. When we look, if we choose to look, at the embroidery panel on the Friends House stairs, we can look through a window on to a long gallery of mirrors, carrying us back from the Friends in Szechwan from whom time and circumstance now separate us, back by stage and again by stage, and again by stage into the remote past of another culture, to far-off, half-glimpsed things. 'The Chinese poet speaks Chinese, but what is it he says?' Of course he says many things which we cannot understand at present; though we can learn more from Arthur Waley's English version of part of the book in his translation called *Monkey*. Here is a glimpse of a supper-party in a Temple, from Chapter Thirteen, when Tripitaka has just started on his quest:

> After supper, sitting by lamp-light, they discussed questions of religion and the purpose of Tripitaka's quest. Some spoke of how wide the rivers were that he must cross, and how high the mountains were that he must climb. Some spoke of the roads being infested by panthers and tigers, some of precipices hard to circumvent and demons impossible to overcome. Tripitaka said nothing, but only pointed again and again at his heart. The priests

29

did not understand what he meant, and when at last they asked him to explain, he said, 'It is the heart alone that can destroy them . . .'[21]

Is it not the very tone of Mr. Valiant-for-Truth in our *Pilgrim's Progress*: 'My sword I give to him that shall succeed me in my pilgrimage, and my courage and skill to him that can get it'?

## 6

The sign over our door has alerted us to the vitality of symbol; the picture on our wall to the nature of myth. No one, I hope, is going to tell me that it is all lies—that there is no Giant Despair and no City of Destruction, when I have lived in the one and lain in the dungeons of the other. So no one is going to tell me either, that although it may be possible to prove that Hsüang-chuang in the seventh century of our era made a long journey from China to India, he was not accompanied by a Stone Monkey, a Pig-Man and a White Horse who was once a Dragon; for I assure you they all went along. I should like to quote some words from a great religious teacher of my lifetime, the Irish poet W. B. Yeats: 'All the great Masters have understood that there cannot be great art without the little limited life of the fable . . . and the rich, far-wandering many-imaged life of the half-seen world beyond it.'[22]

Nor am I ready to accept for a moment that this old Chinese story of which fragments hang on our wall has nothing to say to our very different age. Anything that speaks of greatness of heart speaks to us. 'We are not in ancient bloody classical Greece,' says a character in Tom Stoppard's play *Jumpers*; and we are not in ancient bloody classical China either. Granted, but God forbid that we should be limited to the bloody twentieth century, for that matter. It is, of course, our age; no better and no worse than any other. We must delight to live in it, but not to be imprisoned by it. Anyone who has known the religious experience called 'the communion of saints'—that is, anyone who has felt the living presence of someone from another age, the compulsion of their sweetness, power, eloquence or greatness of heart, has lived outside his own age; and so has anyone who has responded to a sonata of Beethoven, a sonnet of Keats or a painting of Vermeer. True, we make of them what we can, not what they could, in a continuing process of discovery.

If you ask me what has been the most important contribution of the arts to the religious life during the past hundred years, I would say that it has been the re-discovery of the significance of myth—that word which, in the nineteenth century, was the most powerful crowbar of materialism in tearing down the structure of religious faith. It has been my experience that people still anxiously hope that the remains of an actual Ark may be found on a mountain in the Caucasus, want to see pictures of the fallen walls of Jericho, and are fascinated to hear that the Star of Bethlehem may have been a 'nova'. If language reflects our preoccupations—and it does, then the history of the word *myth* is enlightening. The examples of the word given in the Oxford Dictionary all date from the nineteenth century, the first of them in 1830. Much older, however, is the word *mythology*, used before 1600 to describe the interpretations, usually allegorical, of ancient stories; and the adjectives *mythic* and *mythical* which were coined in the seventeenth century, at exactly the same time as *romantic* and *romantical*, to describe the qualities which old stories had for them. In this, the new age of Descartes and the Royal Society, *mythic* became disparaging, a word of contempt for superstition, disguising truth and preventing its discovery. This process had begun even in Greek; *mythos* originally meant something told or spoken 'by word of mouth'. A later word *logos* developed into the word, the truth, even the divine essence (as in the prologue to John's Gospel); while myth became like the Latin *fabula*, a fictional tale, the plot of a play or novel, a professed work of invention or imagination. It was given a special colouring by its use in Plato, with his myths of the origin of Love (in the *Symposium*) and of the Cave (in the *Republic*); and because of Plato's prestige during the Renaissance, and in seventeenth-century England through the Cambridge Platonists, this usage persisted. Nevertheless, the Oxford Dictionary (and other standard works of reference) perpetuate the disparaging use of the word myth:

> a purely fictitious narrative, usually involving super-natural persons, actions, or events, and embodying some popular idea concerning natural or historical phenomena.
> (*Shorter Oxford Dictionary*)

This definition has the double disadvantage of being not only out-of-date but untrue. The myth of Troy reflects an actual siege, the Flood narratives actual floods; the Song of Roland an actual battle (or rather, rearguard skirmish) in the Pyrenees; and our story of Hsüang-chuang an actual journey to the West. Therefore myth is not purely fictional. But the definition also ignores the significance found in the word myth by the romantic movement, and confirmed later by scientific anthropology. This begins with the Brothers Grimm and their probing into folk-lore and fairy-tale (*Kinder und Haus Märchen*, 1809–1822); continues with Max Muller's study of language (1855); develops through field studies and the attempts to codify them in works like Sir James Frazer's *The Golden Bough* (1890); and emerges as a central controversy of modern anthropology. In a field where I have no competence and where much is still controversial, it is essential to my purpose to have a working definition, and I will attempt one, admitting that I blur the distinction between *myth* and *legend*, but claiming that in practice they are rarely kept apart.

> *myth:* The central beliefs of a culture, on which its existence and identity depend, incorporated in narrative form in beings and events, often with a historical core, which are taught as true and reflect the wisdom, needs, pressures and preoccupations of that culture.

But before scientific anthropology or analytical psychology had begun to wrestle with the importance of myth, the artists had become preoccupied with it. William Blake made his own 'Giant forms' from a personal amalgam of the Bible and heretical Jewish lore, Greek and Celtic mythology and the neo-Platonic tradition, mixed with people and places he knew; and however obscure and shadowy these seemed, he was able through them to interpret with startling accuracy the events of his time. Richard Wagner set to work to turn German mythology into 'Music-drama'; and at a time when Wagner was the centre of controversy and the idol of the young all over Europe, his friend Friedrich Nietzsche in collaboration with him, and out of admiration for him, wrote *The Birth of Tragedy from the Spirit of Music*. In it he said:

> Every culture that has lost myth has lost, by the same token, its natural, healthy creativity. Only a horizon ringed round with myths can unify a culture . . . The images of myth must be the daemonic guardians, ubiquitous but unnoticed, presiding over the growth of the child's mind and interpreting to the mature man his life and struggles. Over against this, let us consider abstract man, stripped of myth, abstract education, abstract mores, abstract law, abstract government; the random vagaries of the artistic imagination unchannelled by any native myth, a culture without any fixed and consecrated place of origin, con-

demned to exhaust all possibilities and feed miserably and parasitically on every culture under the sun.[23]

Still under the spell of Wagner, the French poet Stéphane Mallarmé took up the theme in *Richard Wagner, Rêverie d'un poète français*:

> the nineteenth century, or our country that exalts it, has dissolved the myths by thought. Let us remake them.

Later, in 1932, the theme was developed by Antonin Artaud in his series of letters and manifestos known under the collective title of *The Theatre and its Double*:

> The true purpose of the theatre is to create Myths, to express life in its immense, universal aspect, and from that life to extract images in which we can find pleasure in discovering ourselves. And by so doing to arrive at a kind of general resemblance, so powerful that it produces its effect instantaneously. May it free *us*, in a Myth in which we have sacrificed our little human individuality, like Personages out of the Past, with Powers rediscovered in the Past.[24]

And in a phrase used by Jean Cocteau during his *Discours* when he came to take his honorary degree at Oxford in 1956, he summed up the relationship of myth and history:

> Myth is falsehood becoming truth in the long run,
> whereas History is truth becoming falsehood in the
> long run.

Wherever you look for it in modern dance, literature, music, drama or sculpture, you will find myth, though of course there are all sorts of ways of using it. James Joyce took the pattern of the Odyssey and buried it deep beneath the skin of a single day in the lives of Leopold and Molly Bloom and Stephen Dedalus in Dublin—the only clue the title he gave his book, *Ulysses*. W. H. Auden and Christopher Isherwood followed the pattern of folktale in their play *The Dog beneath the Skin*, where the village simpleton sets out to find the missing heir, who is with him all the time in the shape of a shaggy dog. Berthold Brecht stole from China for *The Caucasian Chalk Circle*, and from the mythology of the Thirty Years' War for *Mother Courage*. Richard Strauss and Hofmannsthal mixed classical myth with commedia dell'arte in *Ariadne in Naxos*. Arnold Schoenberg, bolder than most, went straight to the Bible for *Moses and Aaron*, the receiver and transmitter of the message from 'the unimaginable God'. Anouilh re-told *Antigone* in the tense situation of modern war and invasion. Michael Tippett made a myth of his own out of Carl Jung's archetypes; Tolkien out of his study of the ancient Germanic languages. Yeats used Irish myth, and Japanese Nō, and made myths out of the lives of his friends. Benjamin Britten used Lucrece, who came from Livy's *Roman History* via Shakespeare's poem and a play by André Obey. Tom Stoppard used Shakespeare direct, in *Rosencrantz and Guildenstern are dead*, and James Joyce and Oscar Wilde in *Travesties*. Christopher Hampton used genuine South American myths, told straight and very beautifully narrated by Paul Schofield, in *Savages*, as a chorus for a play about the capture of a British diplomat by terrorists.

The weapon which was struck from the hands of religion by nineteenth-century scepticism is restored to us by the gracious gesture of the Muses. Go to Delphi, the gods are still there.

### 7

In a lecture which he gave us on *Poetry and Religious Experience* (in 1948, now reprinted) one of our poets, Clive Sansom, told us that 'Communication may only start when explanation

35

ends'. I think that we should rightly be dissatisfied if this lecture remained content with explanations, and if I could I would like to communicate the nature of my own search and findings by looking with you at a picture; one which employs the confident use of mythology practised during the Renaissance when the Greek gods returned to co-exist happily with the Hebrew mythology of the Bible. The picture I have chosen is by the Venetian master, Titian; and I imagine that most people have seen one of the versions of it, at least in reproduction, even though Titian is at the moment out of fashion (and none the worse for that). I say versions, because Titian painted several; the one I am using is in the Fitzwilliam Museum in Cambridge, and it is now known as *Venus and Cupid with a Lute Player*. The one closest in style is now in the Metropolitan Museum of Art in New York, but for nearly two hundred years it hung at Holkham Hall in Norfolk, and is therefore known as 'The Holkham Venus'; there are other versions, with an organist instead of a lute player. Like many painters, Titian was quite happy to come back to the same subject again and again, but it must clearly have meant much to him, an inexhaustible reservoir of inspiration and meaning.

Titian painted three kinds of pictures during his long life—religious pictures (in the conventionally pious sense), portraits, and those imaginative allegories which he called *poesie*: poem-pictures, if you like. Many of these have recognisable subjects from familiar classical myths, such as Perseus and Andromeda, Bacchus and Ariadne, the death of Actaeon, or Danae and the shower of gold. But a few of them are mysterious and the subject of Venus and the Musician is apparently original, invented by Titian himself. He uses it in celebration of the glory and power of art, linking the world of every day—the most 'earthy'—with the realms of eternity—the spiritual; and that is in part my reason for choosing it, since it lies so close

36

to our theme. Of course, the popularity of Titian's *poesie* in their own time can in part be explained by low motives; they were fashionable, princes liked to own them and carry them from palace to palace (the Holkham Venus still has a fold across it from careless packing, and there is an indignant letter from Philip II of Spain complaining of its state when it reached England, where he was hoping that it would be some consolation to him for the awful climate and the very plain English Queen, Mary Tudor, whom he had to marry for political reasons). The *poesie* were sexy, intended to arouse sensual feelings; and they told a story, sometimes as hard to interpret as a cross-word puzzle—like Victorian 'problem pictures' which cotton magnates liked to own. It is even possible that the model for Venus was one of those famous Venetian courtesans, celebrated throughout Europe for their skill in the improvisation of music: Marietta Bellamo, or the one who called herself Franceschina after the cheeky maid in the Italian comedy. You can't get more down to earth than that, and the great arch of her pale body dominates the right foreground of the picture from her tiny feet through her large thighs and small breasts to her conventionally pretty head. Every wrinkle, curve and dimple of her body is echoed in the wine-dark folds of the curtain draped above her, and the aubergine rug on which she is lying.

In the various versions of the picture, the Goddess of Love (and think how many meanings she has, for a start) is sometimes alone and sometimes, as here, attended by Cupid, that pretty child who, like any child, is so lovable and hurtful. Sometimes she cherishes the symbol of fidelity, a dog; and even the dogs are different—in one version it is a gruff Maltese terrier, in another a bounding, affectionate hound. She wears no clothes, but she wears different jewellery, bracelets and a necklace, sometimes a thin chain of gold, or a ring of pearls.

The musician is sometimes an organist instead of a lutanist; in some versions young (in one the very image of young Philip II himself with his curly hair) and in others middle-aged. Behind them, between the rich gathered folds of the draped curtains, is a landscape—not so much separated by a window as dramatically framed by the looped curtains. Again it varies; sometimes the atmosphere is Alpine and stormy, there are dark woods and distant mountains, sometimes a castle and farms. But in some versions there is a formal, mathematically formal garden, with even rows of poplars in a double avenue, echoing the pipes of an organ on the left-hand side of the composition. Down the avenue stroll an embracing couple enjoying the delights of love; or there are a pair of deer in amorous play, or a peaceful stag. On the right there may be a fountain with a satyr, or a peacock sitting on the rim, or swans on a lake, or nude satyrs dancing in a circle, or a nude man playing a bagpipe as he leans against a tree. The invention never ceases, and if I were Philip of Spain I should want to possess not merely one or two, but all the versions of Venus and the Musician. But let us be content with our Fitzwilliam version. Turner wrote a famous description of it, in which he praised the way in which 'the voluptuous luxury of female charms' is balanced by the landscape which 'insensibly draws the eye away'. We may notice also how the composition is punctuated, as it were, by the disposition of the limbs: like a pair of brackets the left arm of the lutanist fingering his instrument is echoed by the left hand of Venus holding a recorder, and the diminutive left arm of Cupid as he crowns her above.

So now we come to the ironies and ambiguities of the subject. Whatever is going on is going on through all sorts of music; and all sorts of music (as Solomon Eccles kept saying, you remember) imply heavenly as well as earthly music. The recorder

38

in Venus's hand could not be more earthly, for it is made of
metal mined from the earth, 'child of the black earth' as it is
called in an epigram from the Greek Anthology dedicating a
flute to Venus. Yet the creature holding it is heavenly, a divine
being; her unashamed nakedness is the sign of that. A bass
viol stands beside her, its rich brown back one of the colour
keys of the composition; and there is music marked *bassus* for
the viol, and an open music-book labelled *Tenor*, suitable for
the lutanist's voice. So we have lute, recorder, viol and organ;
soprano, tenor and bass. And music is linked with love, in all
the senses of that complicated word. It is love that teaches
music, Erasmus tells us in his *Adagia: musicam docet amor*; and
the sign of the presence of love is the sense of beauty. You can
have it expressed, if you wish, in Edmund Spenser's neo-
Platonism in his *Hymne in honour of Beautie*:

> So every spirit, as it is most pure,
> And hath in it the more of heavenly light,
> So it the fairer bodie doth procure
> To habit in, and it more fairly dight
> With chearfull grace and amiable sight.
> For of the soule the bodie forme doth take:
> For soule is forme, and doth the bodie make.

Or you can have it in Sir Thomas Hoby's Elizabethan translation of Castiglione's dialogue, *The Courtier*, set in the art-loving
court of Urbino and published in Venice when Titian was 51.
Castiglione says of heavenly beauty:

> This is the fiery bush of Moses: the devided tongues of
> fire: the inflamed chariot of Helias (Elijah): which
> doubleth grace and happiness in the soules that be worthie
> to see it, when they forsake this earthly basenesse, and flee
> up to heaven. Let us therefore bend all our force and
> thoughtes of soule to this most holy light.[25]

39

But if you find these Renaissance expressions remote, you can have it in the words of our own Pierre Ceresole:

The Eternal has certainly never yielded to Satan the control of beauty; where beauty is, there the Eternal is in person.[26] (L'Eternel n'a certainement pas cédé à Satan le maniement de la beauté; là où il y a beauté, l'Eternel y est en personne.)

or you can have it in the last long letter which Simone Weil left for Father Perrin when she embarked for the United States, on *Forms of the Implicit Love of God.* 'The beauty of the world,' she says, 'is almost the only way in which we can allow God to penetrate us' and she goes on:

Real love and respect for religious practices are rare even among those who are most assiduous in observing them, and are practically never to be found in others. Most people do not even conceive them to be possible. As regards the supernatural purpose of affliction, compassion and gratitude are not only rare but have become almost unintelligible for almost everyone today. The very idea of them has almost disappeared; the very meaning of the words has been debased.

On the other hand a sense of beauty, although mutilated, distorted and soiled, remains rooted in the heart of man as a powerful incentive. It is present in all the preoccupations of secular life. If it were made true and pure it would sweep all secular life in a body to the feet of God, it would make the total incarnation of the faith possible . . . The beauty of the world is the co-operation of the divine wisdom in creation.[27]

So we return to look again at our picture; for it is through the senses that we enjoy beauty, and in the Renaissance theory of sensation, sight comes first and hearing second. Our vision is physical (we see the picture) but our hearing is spiritual; the goddess has ceased to 'govern the ventages' as Hamlet put it, of her recorder, and looks obliquely beyond us and out of the picture. The man, fallen man (for clothes are the sign of the Fall) dare not face her directly, for divinity is blinding; he turns to glance at her over his shoulder in the only way that a mortal can hope to glimpse transcendent beauty and survive. He is on the left and looks away from us; and castle, forest, garden, fountain, woods, hills and sky are all before him, the beauty of the world, and love in its human and animal senses. She is on the right, with her back to the landscape of earth; but she keeps contact with the physical world by the sense of touch; her foot tickles the musician's back in a gesture which any lover will recognise. The duet in which they have been engaged is amorous as well as musical. For Titian is no Manichean, and in the dialogue of soul and body his conclusion is the same as John Donne's at the end of his poem, *The Extasie*:

> Love's mysteries in soules do grow,
> But yet the body is his booke.

He would not have agreed with Solomon Eccles in seeing the beauty of this world as 'Vanity' to keep us from the truth of heavenly beauty—the devil's trap for the estrangement of our souls.

## 8

When I first joined the Society, the attitude of Solomon Eccles was still to be found among us, though no longer officially approved. In 1936 I was a young actor, involved in organising a season of plays in London which helped to popularise the work of T. S. Eliot, W. H. Auden and Christopher Isherwood, Stephen Spender and Louis MacNeice. I had been warned by Friends, when I went on the stage, that I ran the risk of moral corruption; but when in the autumn of that year Sidcot School mounted a production of *Romeo and Juliet*, I was startled to read in *The Friend* of 13 November 1936 this letter:

> Putting aside the glamour of its being written by Shakespeare, what do we find in 'Romeo and Juliet'? . . . Senseless quarrels, murder, violence, uncontrolled juvenile passion, deceit, suicide, and a spice of the vulgarity of the coarse Elizabethan age. Are these the things on which our children's lives should be moulded? Can the promoters ask the Divine blessing on the successful impersonation of such characters?

> We will not ask the *children*, but were the adults who witnessed the play able to keep it out of their minds at the next Sunday morning meeting? Did not the houses of Montague and Capulet seem more present than 'the things which are lovely and of good report'? I know I am taking the unpopular side, but I would entreat parents and teachers to give the young minds something more wholesome to dwell on than the utterly unreal and disgusting story of Romeo and Juliet.

It is the very tone of Queen Elizabeth's schoolmaster, Roger Ascham, denouncing Malory's *Morte d'Arthur* because it consisted of 'open manslaughter and bold bawdry'. There were weighty replies, started by Maude Brayshaw who thought that we might do worse than meditate on Romeo and Juliet, even in a meeting for worship; but the most powerful answer came from Wilfrid Allott, who said among other things that

> There is a wholeness and beauty and truth in Shakespeare's study of life, beside which even our Quaker classics have a lean and hungry look . . . There is a universe God-made outside the little corner in which we have collected our little collection of the things that are lovely and of good

report . . . In Shakespeare there are depths we never visit
and heights we never reach in ministry, plenary inspiration
of a sincere, intense experience.

Splendid words, still too little heeded among us. But the arts
were becoming a matter of Quaker concern in those years; it
was in the following year, 1937, that Caroline Graveson gave
her Swarthmore Lecture on *Religion and Culture*; and five
passages from that notable lecture have found their way into
the revised version of our *Book of Discipline*.

The impetus for the lecture may have started with a correspondence in *The Friend* four years earlier, which began with a
letter deploring the absence of the arts from the Swarthmore
Lectures. The correspondence went on through June and
July of 1933, and among those who took part was the sculptor
Eric Gill, who contrasted the Catholic attitude of acceptance
('The Catholic Church takes man in general; she omits nothing,
refuses nothing') with Protestant stuffiness: 'Many people
look askance at man's delight in making.' It is interesting
that Joseph Southall (the painter who wanted to decorate
Friends House) refused to take the proposal seriously, 'I feel
sure it would provide a pleasant topic for teatime', while the
writer Doris Dalglish thought it a pity to contemplate, and
told us roundly that 'Art has no message—and we place the
artists on too high a pedestal'. Others were against art as
Coolidge's preacher was against sin; and one correspondent
narrowed the accusation against *contemporary* artists who, he
said specifically, had no religious message: 'With the notable
exception of T. S. Eliot, Eric Gill and a few composers, our
artists to-day cannot be called religious.'

It seems to me that it is there that our modern heresy lies,
for I believe the contrary. It seems to me, for a start, that
there are few important composers who are *not* religious,

43

starting with Wagner, and Brahms, and Mahler who described
his Third Symphony as 'a musical poem embracing all the
stages of development step by step. It begins with inanimate
nature and rises to the love of God.' Then there are the
obviously religious British composers, Elgar, Vaughan-
Williams and Holst; but the controversially 'modernist'
composers of the early century are emphatic in their claims.
As early as 1912 Arnold Schoenberg, writing to the Austrian
poet Richard Dehmel about an oratorio he was contem-
plating, but which he left unfinished at his death in 1951,
gave this description of *Jacob's Ladder* (Die Jakobsleiter):

> For a long time I have been wanting to write an oratorio
> on the following subject: modern man, having passed
> through materialism, socialism and anarchy, and despite
> having been an atheist, still having in him some residue
> of ancient faith (in the form of superstition) wrestles with
> God (see also Strindberg's *Wrestling Jacob*) and finally
> succeeds in finding God and becoming religious. Learning
> to pray!
>
> It is *not* through any action, any blows of fate, least of all
> through any love of woman, that this change of heart is
> to come about. Or at least, these should be no more than
> hints in the background, giving the initial impulse. And
> above all, the mode of speech, the mode of thought, the
> mode of expression, should be those of modern man;
> the problems treated should be those that harass us. For
> those who wrestle with God in the Bible also express
> themselves as men of their own time, speaking of their
> own affairs, remaining within their own social and intel-
> lectual limits. That is why, though they are artistically
> impressive, they do not offer a subject for a modern
> composer who fulfils his obligations . . . I could never
> shake off the thought of 'Modern Man's Prayer'.[28]

44

All his life Schoenberg wrestled with the 'unimaginable God' as he travelled through the desert of sickness and neglect; we are concerned, he said in his *Harmonielehre*, with 'a premonition concealed in dazzling mystery'. Then there is Alban Berg, with his compassion for the sufferings of the lowest. And Leos Janacek: 'You know what they wrote about me,' he said on the occasion of his *Glagolitic Mass*, 'The old man who believes in God. This made me cross, and I said, "Young man, in the first place I am not old, and a believer in God, not at all; no, not at all". Until I had found out the opposite.' And in reply to an address from the Ostrava musical societies he wrote down his creed:

> Grow out of your innermost selves.
> Never renounce your beliefs.
> Do not toil for recognition;
> But always do all you can
> So that the field allotted to you
> May prosper.[29]

Stravinsky dedicated his *Symphony of Psalms* 'To the glory of God'; and Michael Tippett said 'The moral of *The Midsummer Marriage* is enlightenment.'

Without multiplying more examples from the composers, let us turn to the writers. I suppose that in 1933 the ex-Congregationalist D. H. Lawrence, who had died three years earlier, was still regarded as an enemy to religion by many people. But I should like to know where, among the theologians of the day, the central truth of religion, the sense of its living presence, was conveyed as freshly, sincerely, or immediately as in Lawrence's attack on Benjamin Franklin in *Studies in Classic American Literature*, published in 1924:

> The religious truth is the same now as it has ever been:
> that preceding all our knowledge or will or effort is the

central creative mystery, out of which issues the strange and for ever unaccountable emanation of creation: that the universe is a bush which burns for ever with the Presence, consuming itself and yet never consumed . . . the Presence, never to be located, yet never to be doubted, because it is *always* evident to our living soul, the Presence from which issues the first fine shaken impulse and prompting of new being, eternal creation which is always Now.[30]

One of the first group of 'Absurd' playwrights after the Second World War was Arthur Adamov, whom Friends had rescued from a camp in the south of France. In his Confession (*L'Aveu*, dated Paris 1938) he said:

What is there? I know first of all that I am. But who am I? All I know of myself is that I suffer. And if I suffer, it is because at the origin of myself there is mutilation, separation. I am separated. What I am separated from—I cannot name it. But I am separated. (*and in a footnote:*) Formerly it was called God. Today it no longer has a name.[31]

In the dark days of the Vietnam War there appeared in the streets of America a company who gave short plays of protest. They called themselves The Bread and Puppet Theatre, and their costumes and masks, their great twelve-foot high puppets, were made from scrap which they salvaged from the streets; their shows often began with a distribution of bread to the audience, an assuagement of hunger, a Holy Communion. One of their plays, *Fire*, was dedicated (among others) to Norman Morrison, the Friend who burnt himself to death on the steps of the Pentagon in protest against the burning of Vietnamese children. Someone who saw the play wrote that 'it has the quality of prayer' and then bravely tried to define what that meant to him. It seems to me that no priest in our time has so tenderly and profoundly investigated the depths of prayer as this agnostic to whom it was only 'a childhood memory':

> I remember things like these: a peopling of death with human forms, a vague yet affecting sense of the scale of things; a notion of the preciousness of life, and of its vulnerability; a touch of fear, since fate is everywhere and has little to do with one's wishes . . . In some senses Schumann's play (*Fire*) is like a dream. The dream does not express emotion, but pulls us deeply into the matrix of emotion . . . Finally it releases us, and we feel that we have conceived a prayer for the victims of this world.[32]

It seems to me that Quakers would prefer not to be reminded of the death of Norman Morrison; there is, for instance, no file about him anywhere in Friends House; but the story of his martyrdom appeared in two plays: Peter Schumann's *Fire* and Peter Brook's *US* at the Aldwych Theatre. I hope therefore, now that I have mentioned it, that I shall not have to face the criticism that there are more important matters than art for a Swarthmore Lecture. Artaud said in 1938 that he wanted to extend the frontiers of what is called 'reality' by seeking 'in the mysterious depths of ourselves' (which would be no bad definition of a Quaker meeting); and that when he spoke the word 'life' he was 'not referring to life as we know it from the surface of fact, but to that fragile, fluctuating centre which forms never reach'. He admitted that the world is not concerned with 'culture' but with hunger, and that it would be artificial to try and turn towards 'culture' the thoughts that are occupied with hunger. He didn't want a culture which left men hungry, but he did want to 'extract from what is called culture, ideas whose compelling force is identical with that of hunger'. In the arts we find those *ideas whose compelling force is identical with that of hunger,* and we starve for lack of them. To find religion in our time we may have to look in strange places. I don't know where I would look to find something closer to my own strivings than in the plays of Tom Stoppard, especially *Jumpers,* with its desperately pathetic and comic search for God among the ruins of a marriage, a civilisation and an academic discipline disparaged and despised; and *Travesties,* with its discussion farcical, and therefore serious, of the nature and importance of art itself.

## 9

I have named in this lecture great masters, whose fame hangs so heavy on them that it is hard to decide sometimes whether it is a golden chain of honour or an iron chain of impediment. I have also named controversial figures in the modern movement, to whom the reader's attitude may be one of impatient dismissal—finding their plays truly absurd, their poems meaningless, their compositions mere cacophony. But now I turn to my own humble efforts, in the hope that by describing my stumbling steps, I may give occasion for the reader to smile and take comfort. For art is an activity that operates at all levels, and masterpieces are the incidental by-products of its ferment.

I began, like most people, with the magic worlds of folk-tale and nursery-rhyme; but I differ from some in feeling that they have never left me, and that they still comfort, warm and warn me. I agree with Joseph Campbell in calling them 'the primer of the picture-language of the soul'. I grew up with poems good and bad, and loved both equally. I had the whole of Tennyson's *The Lady of Shalott* by heart before I was nine, and stood up to recite it to the whole school. Obedient as

children were in those days, I don't believe I would have got
through it, or been allowed to try, if I had not found my way
instinctively to something of the performer's art. I feel now,
sixty years later, that I did understand it then: the lady's
desire for, and terror of experience, the power of fantasy and
its danger. I can remember some of it still, though I confess I
have checked my recollection by the book:

> She left the web, she left the loom,
> She took three paces through the room,
> She saw the water-lily bloom,
> She saw the helmet and the plume,
>    She look'd down to Camelot.
> Out flew the web and floated wide;
> The mirror crack'd from side to side
> 'The curse is come upon me,' cried
>    The Lady of Shalott.

The other, equally loved but I am afraid bad poem, was *The
Highwayman* by Alfred Noyes—what a rollicking ride that was:

> The road was a ribbon of moonlight, over the purple moor
> And the highwayman came riding, riding, riding—
>    The highwayman came riding,
>    up to the old inn door.

I am sure that then, one did as much for me as the other; it
was only later that one continued to speak, and the other had
nothing to say. But we should never be ungrateful or deny
past experience; for me, it echoes with the pounding of hooves
and the shining tresses of Bess, the landlord's daughter,
'plaiting a dark-red love knot into her long black hair'.

Next came Shakespeare; and it fills me with horror to hear
that in a quiz at Winchester he was recently voted 'the most
boring writer'. I would rather agree with Anthony Burgess,

who calls him 'one of our redeemers'. I have loved him from my first play, *A Midsummer Night's Dream* at Lilian Baylis's Old Vic, through the bliss—do you hear, Winchester, the *bliss* of school lessons on *Hamlet*—to the first sampling of the mysterious late romances in Perdita's speech at the sheep-shearing feast in *The Winter's Tale*. I could not then have read or understood this play of redemption from bitter and destructive jealousy; I did not know the context of what I found quoted in an old book in my father's study. I did not need to learn it, it entered my heart instantly and without effort while I stood there; but don't ask me to repeat it, for the thought of it reduces me to tears.

With music I had a more mixed initiation. My adventurous mother went from a Yorkshire mining town into the service of a Roman princely family. She had begun to learn singing from an Italian teacher in Leeds, and in Italy she took lessons in *bel canto* from the best Roman masters of her day; she had a sweet and true, though not large or florid voice. Her repertoire was indiscriminate; it included oratorio and drawing-room ballads, musical comedy airs and popular Italian songs of the day. She sang them all with equal gusto, from 'Home, sweet home' to 'Funiculi, Funicula'; and although I enjoyed them, I found to my own dismay that I began to feel their inadequacy. Her accompanist was a neighbour, who used to sing Schubert and Schumann lieder in a small thin voice as he played them, in a way that spoke to me. I had learnt a little German from my father's Viennese friends, and I was beginning to play the violin—simplified airs from Händel and Corelli were my introduction to baroque music. I now began, with my fiddle and scrap of voice, to go through the Schubert albums from end to end. It was a very intimate matter between Schubert and me—the time often wrong, the violin not always in tune, and rarely a pianist to accompany me. There was no degree of

50

musical attainment in it, no skill, no heady sense of achieve-
ment—only a passionate intimacy. It was years before I heard
any lieder properly sung by Elena Gerhardt or Schwarzkopf
or Fischer-Dieskau; yet some of my deepest experiences lie
there; and I knew, as I have always known, that beyond the
instant appeal of *An die Musik* or *Gretchen am spinnrad* there
was always more to seek, more beyond my range; I have never
had patience with those who are content with what they have
found.

With the visual arts it was different again; it is still a daunt-
ing thought that I might take brush in hand, though my mother
and her friends painted in oils and the Suffolk farmer whom I
helped in harvest time used to go off when the sheaves were
'safely gathered in' to paint water-colours in the East Anglian
tradition. I had no confidence that I might do it myself, though
twice in adult life I have been challenged to do so. Once was
while I was teaching briefly at Corsham, the Bath Academy of
Art. I was talking with a colleague, Stephen Russ, knowing
nothing of his close involvement with Friends in German
relief after the First World War. He said nothing about that,
but suddenly he said, 'Why don't you come over and do some
fabric printing?' Me! Fabric printing! Me, make an ass of
myself in front of those students I was supposed to impress!
I committed the crime against the Holy Ghost and refused the
proffered opportunity; but I was given a second chance. At
a summer conference of the Quaker Fellowship of the Arts
Howard Pickersgill thrust half a potato into my hand and told
me to make a printing block out of it. This time I did not
refuse, and suddenly felt released; and I tell you this story so
that you in turn may not refuse the blessings that God sends
you through the hands of your friends. I want to share with
you that sense of the importance of bad art as well as good.
Art as an activity matters, however the product be judged.

51

I am for ephemeral art—for the song of the moment, for all that comforts and entertains, for doggerel birthday wishes, for the skit at the summer school social, and for the touching memorial verses at the back of the local paper, made by the family so that Gran may go with dignity, and the deep feeling find some memorial beyond a bunch of flowers.

Of course in art, as in any other field of life from food to morals, we must learn to discern and to discriminate; but distinctions become blasphemous when they are used to exclude anything except what is bad in its place and among its own kind. Let no one set 'folk art' against 'high art', amateur against professional, 'realistic' against 'abstract', 'classical' music against 'pop', 'traditional' painting against 'modern' or worse 'modernistic' or worst of all 'ultra-modern', and let us dispense altogether with those ugly words 'highbrow' and 'lowbrow'. Past examples should teach us the danger: seventeenth-century critics spoke of the 'rough music' of Chaucer's verse knowing nothing of its principles, and condemned Shakespeare's plays for their lack of 'unity', meaning their own kind of unity; Victorian critics dismissed Donne's poems as 'incomprehensible'; and twentieth-century critics condemned the 'mindlessness' of jazz, and the 'filth' of Molly Bloom's great poem of affirmation at the end of Joyce's *Ulysses*.

I learnt about pretence in my teens. My father, in order to provide us with continental holidays, became a travel courier and a very successful one; we sometimes travelled with parties of fifty or more through the cities of Italy and Austria. In the Uffizi Gallery in Florence, or the Albertina in Vienna, where the world's masterpieces were set before us, I watched our parties trudge dutifully from room to room and heard the repeated desolate moan: '*When* are we going to get a cup of tea?' They wanted to be able to say that they had been there, but they were going the wrong way to get the experience.

I felt an exile among the Philistines; but I was soon to learn the precariousness of my own taste.

I went with a hard-won scholarship to Cambridge, and found myself in the same college as Alistair Cooke and on the same staircase as J. Bronowski (for in those days he hid his Biblical forename behind an initial, and answered to the pet name of Bruno. Being poor, he wrote all his early poems on my typewriter, a twenty-first birthday present which I hardly saw from one term's end to the other). Bruno was then better known as a poet than as an expositor of science, and his circle included William Empson, Kathleen Raine, T. H. White and Richard Eberhart; while over in Oxford, as we were jealously aware, rose the rival star of Wystan Auden. I went to Cambridge full of the Georgian poets enshrined in that famous (or infamous) anthology, *Poems of Today*, only to find that I knew none of the right names: it was down with Tennyson and up with Donne, down with Rupert Brooke and up with T. S. Eliot. I was face to face with 'modern art'; and soon after I went down from the University, having succeeded Alistair Cooke as president of one of the University dramatic societies, I found myself involved with T. S. Eliot and Wystan Auden in creating that 'modern art' which provoked such howls of rage.

In old age I can say that I like Rupert Brooke—not better than Eliot or Auden, for in my sincere judgment he is not as good a poet as either—but Blake was right, 'None are greatest in the Kingdom of Heaven, it is so in Poetry.' If intellectual snobbery is a vice it has this virtue, that it drives you to master what you only pretend to know and love, if only from the fear of being found out. Would I ever have got what I did from *The Waste Land* if I had not pretended to be as worldly and sophisticated as Bronowski at the top of the stairs? Would I not have missed one of the chief pleasures of my life if I had not wanted to be one of the few who could read medieval French poems in the original? There are base motives that are just as valuable as our virtuous leadings—and don't always do more harm. The chief conundrum of my life, which I shall now never resolve, is why my good intentions have so often been disastrous, and my base and selfish acts occasionally so fruitful. In my pursuit of virtue I fear I began at the wrong end and so never reached it, but in my too rare selfishness I acted like an honest man and satisfied myself; and a satisfied person is rich and safe. Ask Blake again:

> Abstinence sows sand all over
> The ruddy limbs and flaming hair,
> But Desire gratified
> Plants fruits of life and beauty there.

Meanwhile, I had joined the Society of Friends. I began attending meeting before I went to Cambridge; and I think the first time I ever gave a talk for Friends was in a study group in Hammersmith Meeting (where one member, Emily Dowling, to whose memory I pay grateful tribute, prophesied that I would one day give the Swarthmore Lecture). For half a century since that time I have spoken for Friends on all sorts of subjects and in all sorts of settings, from remote country meetings to church pulpits, and even among the lions in Trafalgar Square. But not until 1976 was I ever asked by the Society to share those things which meant most to me, my experience of the arts. At last, at the end of my life I can atone for an act of apostasy, and speak from the centre of myself instead of the periphery; I hope I make clear why I feel that you have failed me, and that I have failed you, and why I am so deeply grateful to the Swarthmore Lecture Committee for proposing this subject.

In the meeting at Hammersmith, in that beautiful old house

by the river, where I learned so much and met so many lovely people, there was indeed an artistic presence. There were people who had known my 'man of men', William Morris, who had lived close by. There were four professional painters, including the Academician Bertram Priestman and the enchanting, shy cosmopolitan Estella Canziani, whose romantic house on the edge of Kensington Gardens was full of treasures, and provided the title for her scatty, charming autobiography, *Number Three, Palace Green*. At the head of the meeting sat my close friend and mentor, ninety-year-old Mary Elizabeth Bennett, who as a child had walked hand in hand with William Wordsworth. In such an atmosphere, surely the arts must have taken a natural and inevitable place, and must have been spoken of with knowledge and love?

I never heard any of the painters use their experience or share their vision in ministry. I heard fervent prayer, but I never heard any of them pray, as my actress friend Flora Robson told us she did, every night, 'Lord, make me a better actress'—exhorting us to do the same. Subjects for our study groups never included music, poetry or drama; and the painters never hotly discussed those schools which then divided the world of painting—Impressionism, Expressionism, Fauvism, Cubism, Surrealism—although we could have begun with *Vision and Design* by Ruth and Joan Mary Fry's brother, Roger Fry, the leading art critic of the time. Poets appeared in the Adult School syllabus, but they were the 'safe' poets, Browning and Wordsworth, not any of those then hot from the press—the later Yeats, Edwin Muir, T. S. Eliot or Ezra Pound—who excited me.

My two worlds were completely segregated, and I am startled now to think how hermetically sealed from each other they were. I knew that Roger Fry and Annie Horniman (of the Manchester Rep. and the Abbey Theatre) had been brought up as Friends, but had left us. I knew that many important writers had at some time come within the Quaker orbit, but never into membership. There was Dorothy Richardson, whose name I mentioned in literary lecture courses as one of the creators of the 'stream of consciousness' school of novelists; she wrote a book about us, and like her heroine Miriam, attended our meetings which she lovingly described. There was Aldous Huxley, whom I met and whose *Perennial Philosophy* showed the range of his religious search; and there was Auden, who had taught at a Quaker school and had dedicated one of his best early poems to his headmaster Geoffrey Hoyland:

> Equal with colleagues in a ring
> I sit on each calm evening
>  Enchanted as the flowers
> The opening light draws out of hiding
> With all its gradual dove-like pleading,
>  Its logic and its powers:
>
> That later we, though parted then,
> May still recall these evenings, when
>  Fear gave his watch no look;
> The lion griefs loped from the shade
> And on our knees their muzzles laid,
>  And Death put down his book.[33]

I never spoke to any of them of the Society of Friends; any more than I spoke to Friends about them. But I can guess their reactions from those of our good friend and partner in many adventures of the spirit, Maude Royden: 'I find Friends defective in their appreciation of beauty, and I find that they imagine this defect to be a virtue'. Or Vera Brittain, when asked at the end of the war in 1945 to write an article on 'Why I am not a Friend' said, with regret, that 'I have not found . . .

56

that by joining the Society of Friends, a would-be creative artist *can avoid becoming a less significant artist*, in the endeavour to achieve the moral status of a social philanthropist.' Dorothy Richardson's own verdict was strikingly similar: she was kept out by the sense of her 'inability to engage in social enterprise' though she felt most affinity with the Quakers; but 'the artist's link with religion is nearly quite entirely aesthetic . . . and therefore they won't have us inside'. To come nearer home, I do not know who has expressed what I feel better than Pleasaunce Holtom, who in an article in *Reynard*, the magazine of the Quaker Fellowship of the Arts, wrote in 1975 that she felt there was still 'a subtle lack of recognition for the arts' in our Society. She described the attempt 'to find in creative activity an experience that is essentially religious, but doesn't need to use the debased currency of religious language'. She found that 'the passionate involvement in visual discoveries seemed incompatible with a dull round of committees concerned with good works' and she asked 'Where would I have been without older Friends to introduce me to Blake, give me Keats's letters to read, play Bach to me, or show me Rembrandt's drawings?'

The arts are now admitted, but as an *amenity* and not as a *necessity*, with mild pleasure rather than passionate intensity, as a relief from life's pressures rather than as a way of harnessing them.

## 10

Everyone knows the prayer with which John Wilhelm Rowntree ended the great Manchester Conference of 1895: 'Lay on us the burden of the world's suffering'. It is a Titan's prayer, which few of us are truly qualified to pray; but the experience of art contains something of it. It needs, if we are to survive, to be balanced by another prayer of equal validity and importance: 'Grant us an experience of the world's joy'. Though this may appear to be easier, yet for religious people, especially those bred in the Protestant tradition, it often seems inaccessible and has indeed often been taught as undesirable: the world's joy is that 'Vanity' of which Solomon Eccles, Fox and Barclay were so suspicious. I must admit, and I hate to do so, that their suspicion has been bred in me; and therefore I pray this prayer for myself and others with the same intensity as John Wilhelm Rowntree felt on that great occasion, in the shadow of his own threatened powers and early death. It is not something light and trivial that we are asking, nor is it something distinct from suffering; it co-exists with tragedy in *King Oedipus* and *King Lear*, in Beethoven's last quartets and in Picasso's savage *Guernica*. It has a name: that name is delight; it is something that goes to the heart, to the source of life itself, and tells us that beyond good and ill, all is well. There is a hymn to delight in our Book of Discipline, addressed by Francis Howgill to the memory of his friend Edward Burrough, the first of our leaders to die in 1663 in Newgate Gaol:

> The Kingdom of Heaven did catch and gather us all as in a net . . . inasmuch that we often said to one another with great joy of heart, What, is the Kingdom of God come to be with men ?[34]

To meet that sense today, we might more profitably look outside our own tradition to the Quakers of Kenya or India; I am thinking of Margaret Snyder's wonderful description of a meeting with Gurdial Mallik in 1965:

> I was the guest of my dear friend Raihana in New Delhi. Raihana ran to call me, all alight with joy in his coming, and the whole household was filled with laughter and gladness. I remember how he sat, feet tucked under him,

on the foot of Raihana's couch talking with a gaiety and tenderness that animated each person present. At Raihana's suggestion he told us the laughter-filled story of his prolonged effort to become a member of London Yearly Meeting—from the evening in a Bombay garden when an inner voice told him he should join the Society of Friends . . . There was only Love, no faintest echo of malice or resentment in that story . . . That day's encounter opened my heart to a fresh knowing of what the glory of sainthood means. He seemed a being compounded altogether of Light, so undiluted that when I remember that day I feel my own too-often obscured light released to the kind of glad playfulness which sparkled in his presence.[35]

You recognise that feeling, I am sure; for everyone has felt delight, though they might not use so pretentious a word for an everyday experience which the slightest occasion may evoke —a child running in the street, a leaf blowing in the autumn wind, the goal that wins a football match, or reunion after long absence. But the experience of delight is incarnate in art; and I use the word incarnate with reverent intention, because art belongs to both worlds, visible and invisible; it is the gift of grace.

But there is a dark and searching side to it as well; a penitential journey.

## 11

Many stories are told of the wise King Solomon, son of David, in Jewish, Christian and Islamic lore. Some of the most persistent, found in all countries of Europe including Russia, tell of his encounters with a kind of alter ego who goes by various names: Marcolf, Morolf, or even Saturn (and for clarity we will use the last and most familiar name, which occurs in the oldest known versions, two Anglo-Saxon dialogues of the ninth century). One of these is a kind of wit-contest or 'flighting' in which riddles and gnomic remarks are exchanged, with Solomon standing for Christian wisdom, and Saturn for the pagan learning of the East. In later forms, the opponent does not play the part of oriental wisdom, but of the 'Sancho Panza view of life', as George Orwell called it— the 'voice of the belly protesting against the soul', the subversive humour of the underdog, peasant or artisan, contemptuous of ideals, despising authority whether of church or state.

So there sits Solomon in all his glory, and in comes this coarse mis-shapen clown with his sluttish wife. Solomon accepts his challenge to a trial of wisdom, and promises him great rewards if he wins. Every proverb or wise aphorism which the King proposes is countered by some coarse or ridiculous parallel, parody or counterpart. At last the King is exhausted, but refuses his courtiers' advice to throw out Saturn, even if he has to give him best for the time being. The series of bouts continues, some of them set in the churl's hut in the forest. The subjects become more and more absurd. Saturn asserts that milk is not whiter than daylight, that you can't trust a woman, that nature is stronger than nurture—and goes to all lengths to prove his point. Solomon has a princely cat of which he is very proud, it has been trained to sit at table and hold a lighted candle between its paws, proving that nature can be overcome by nurture—you can even overcome an animal's instinctive fear of fire. Saturn arrives with a pocketful of live mice and throws them, one by one, in front of the cat. At the third mouse, the cat throws down the candle and gives chase.

Quakers too have had their King Solomons and their Queen Esthers, with all the presence of reigning monarchs, and such wisdom and sanctity as even the Pope of Rome might acknowledge. We too have gloried in the triumphs of nurture over nature, holding the candle of the Lord and watching the mice scutter one by one into the wainscot. But we do not always seem prepared, like Solomon the great King, to accept the challenge of the churl and his sluttish wife, to engage in wit-combat with them, to go to their hut in the forest and fall into the pan of milk set to trap us. One can see George Fox be-spattered with milk as he was with mire on many occasions; but although he had his own po-faced brand of humour, he could not abide 'light, chaffy men'. Do you remember the captain of horse in Weymouth who was

> the fattest, merriest, cheerfullest man and the most given to laughter that ever I met with; so that I several times was moved of the Lord to speak to him in the dreadful power of the Lord. And yet he would presently after laugh at anything he saw; and I still admonished him to sobriety and the fear of the Lord and sincerity.[36]

Well, after a night at the inn the merry captain could stand no more, and he left George Fox; but the next time George saw him he confessed that 'the power of the Lord had so amazed him that before he got home he was serious enough and left his laughing'. What a pity, what a very great pity; humour is among the sharpest of spiritual tools.

We have been reminded lately of the masks worn by public men, and the fact that private men (and women) wear them too. John Reith confessed that he discovered too late that 'life is for living'; Paul Tillich's widow tells the world that he was sensual and selfish as well as a great theologian and an adorable man (why should we be surprised?); and it is a relief to know from his diaries that Gladstone, that pillar of Victorian recti-tude, did not fool himself about the nature of his interest in the prostitutes whom he tried (in vain) to rescue from the streets of London. Closest of all to us is the story of our own Richard Nixon whom we bred and raised and fed with good example and the word of God. His public unctuousness and industry—all we taught him—are balanced by the deleted expletives of the Watergate tapes, and the intricacies of the 'dirty tricks' department. Blake saw the danger: 'Attempting to be more than Man, We become less.'

There are too many Friends with whom I, at least, feel driven to put on that solemn face which George Fox asked of the merry captain. In her lecture last year, Damaris Parker-Rhodes said a very severe thing which, to me, struck home: 'Many religious people never come to possess their inner selves, and they use their form of worship as a vaccination to keep them safe from living experience.' That living experience includes very dark places; and yet it is the revelation and examination of those dark places which people most resent in modern literature and drama, and dread to find and face in themselves.

One of the most unexpected and successful missionaries in the days of the Friends Foreign Mission Association was George Swan. He came from a family of 'mumpers' who travelled the fairgrounds of England with a nigger minstrel troupe, and at eight years old his elders found it fun to make him drunk. I love to think of him in India, sitting at sundown like a father among the weavers of Itarsi; or wandering with his fiddle among the hill-tribes, picking up Indian songs. He once said, 'I think my early life helped me to understand some sorts of people in a style I couldn't any other way. Carefully-brought up Friends are too innocent by half. They simply don't know what some things mean'.

The situation hasn't changed very much in a hundred years. But the arts could help us to explore the human situation, 'to teach the human heart a knowledge of itself', which is Laurence

Olivier's definition of the function of drama. The other half
of King Lear is King Lear's Fool.

## 12

I have shared with you a picture, let me share with you also
a poem which seems to me to sum up what I have been saying
with a perfection inaccessible to me. It is called *The Iron Coin*,
and we must ask why—for though iron has its value, we depend
on it every day, but not for making coins (it rusts, it is too
heavy, it is not 'precious'). Like all coins, it has two sides;
'heads' is for the poet a 'pure labyrinth' in whose symbolism
he sees Adam, the 'young Paradise', 'God in every creature'.
But 'tails', when we toss it again 'is no one and nothing and
darkness and blindness'—that shadow side of human nature.
The poem is one of human love, and in that love the two sides
of our nature both appear. The poem is by the great poet of
Argentina, Jorge Luis Borges:

### The Iron Coin (*La Moneda de Hierro*)

Here is the iron coin. Let us ask
The two opposing faces what will be the answer
To the obstinate question that no one has not asked
    himself:
Why does a man require that a woman should love him?
Let us see. On the upper sphere are interwoven
The fourfold firmament borne up by the flood
And the unalterable planets.
Adam, the young father, and the young Paradise.
The evening and the morning. God in every creature.
In this pure labyrinth is your reflection.

Let us toss again the iron coin
Which is also a magic mirror. Its reverse side

63

Is no one and nothing and darkness and blindness. That
is you.
The two faces forge a single iron echo.
Your hands and your tongue are unfaithful witnesses.
God is the ungraspable centre of the ring.
He neither praises nor condemns. He behaves better: he
forgets.
Falsely charged with infamy, why should they not love
you?
In the darkness of the other we seek our darkness;
In the glass of the other, our necessary glass.[37]

## 13

At this stage, when I have almost done, I look back anxiously
at the committee's briefing, to see if I have done as I was bidden.
I was asked, in the first place, to say as far as I could, how God
can be discovered through the arts. I hope that all I have written
is my answer. There are few human activities in which perfection is possible; for in most things the human limitations of
knowledge, time, energy, skill, and motive impede us; only in
the arts do they work for us, so that we can truly say of certain
works of music, poetry, painting, sculpture and architecture
that we can neither wish nor imagine them otherwise. When we
find this degree of perfection and are able to respond to it,
they become in sober truth a revelation of the divine in the
sense that Jesus was: human yet complete.

There are also very few human activities in which honesty is
possible. Try as we may, we are blinded by prejudice, by
circumstance, by ignorance, by upbringing, by self-deception—
or even by the excellence and thoroughness of the education
and training which teach us to look for certain patterns and
to assume certain attitudes. Artists are not more perfect than

other men, sometimes, indeed, less so. But in their art it is a different matter; their lips are touched with coals of fire. This honesty deserves, and commands, our trust.

But of course, works of this quality, bought at the price of all that a man has, are the peaks of giant pyramids, in which we pass our time, if at all, on the lowest slopes. When I turn my attention to the other part of my brief—that 'I should feel free to urge upon the Society a wider use of these modes of experience if I consider them as a suitable development for Quaker life'—we have then to labour at the base; it is as if we turned away from *Isaiah* or Mark's Gospel to some minute rules in *Leviticus*. But with no base there can be no peaks; with no scales, no sonatas. The miracles of German music arise from innumerable choral societies and back-street string quartets.

Since the first reactions to any suggestions show anxiety lest our spontaneous and 'silent' worship should be in danger, let me reassure you; it is not. But if the 'silence' includes speech, prayer or reading, it can—and sometimes does—include song, where this is appropriate and spontaneous. Might this not sometimes come (for instance) from a girl with a guitar? And since many meetings now, in practice, acknowledge the great feasts of the year—Christmas and Easter, often with readings and music outside the regular time of worship—why can we not formally and officially accept such meetings? Ours is a religion of experience; and it has been the experience of those of us who, during recent Yearly Meetings have joined in music-worship groups, that they can be a deep and true form of Quaker worship. When, at the 'pop' sessions late at night during the York residential Yearly Meeting we heard also spoken ministry from the young who are usually silent in our meetings or absent from them, we felt justified, helped by the very informal sincerity of the occasion.

In looking for more acceptance of the arts among us, the first signs of life I should look for would be very humble ones. We should see, for example, in Quaker homes more evidence of positive taste. I do not mean *my* taste, but any kind of taste that was personal and passionate. Then I should like to see something of the love expended on Monthly Meeting teas reflected in the standard of food offered at Friends House; and again, I am not asking for cordon bleu booking, but for a marginal improvement, a sense that it matters, in a spiritual sense, what and how we eat. Then, about three times a year, I should like to see an item of any kind about the arts finding a place on the agenda of the Meeting for Sufferings; I cannot remember there ever being one. There are General Meetings which occasionally turn their sessions into workshops for the arts; let this become more common. When concerts are given in our meeting-houses, let them sometimes be for the music's sake, and not to raise money for charity. Let us think, as a distant possibility, of providing as much money annually for the arts as for the smaller of our present standing committees; that is (on the 1978 budget estimates) about £40,000. Some of this money we could use, year by year, for an artist in residence: one year a painter, sculptor, or graphic designer, another a writer, another a musician—or once in a way, a small group of musicians. They could be chosen from students leaving the established academies and schools of art; they might be attached to the General Meeting putting up the most interesting offer of work and hospitality, and they would be available also for national gatherings, week-ends and summer schools. Part of the money would also be used from time to time to assist young Friends to travel to see works of art or to take part in artistic activities. Once in a way it would be used to purchase a work of art—a painting or piece of sculpture—for Friends House or for a new Meeting-house opened in that year. A proportion would be set aside to enable Meeting-house libraries to buy books on art. The fund would give account of its stewardship to Yearly Meeting, and once every few years a session of Yearly Meeting would be set aside for the consideration of some aspect of contemporary art, with the help if necessary of outside experts. But in none of these things should we look specifically for 'religious' art—it is on the contrary in art that ranges most widely that we shall find food for our souls, an enlargement of our vision.

## 14

Quakerism has long exercised the *knowing* faculty, to the profit of mankind and in reverent contemplation of the works of God. Our striking contributions in various fields of science and technology have been the subject of generous praise from outside our borders, and of frequent comment in this series of lectures. Now, in the technological wonderland we have helped to create, we walk about like lost children, sometimes admiring, then suddenly intimidated; hoping that the machines may prove to be friendly—but very, very anxious that they may not.

In this situation, we might listen to what one of the great Victorian scientists had to say. A landmark in the religious debate of that age was the 'Belfast Address' delivered to the British Association for the Advancement of Science at its meeting in Belfast in 1874, by John Tyndall, once on the staff of our Friend George Edmondson's Queenwood College in Hampshire, and later Michael Faraday's successor at the Royal Institution. You might suppose from references to it in the literature of the time, that Tyndall's Belfast Address was a mortal blow in the side of religious orthodoxy; but judge for yourself from the peroration, which ought to be delivered in the full splendour of an Irish voice:

> The inexorable advance of man's understanding in the path of knowledge, and *those unquenchable claims of his moral and emotional nature which the understanding can never satisfy*, are here equally set forth. The world embraces not only a Newton but a Shakespeare,—not only a Boyle but a Raphael—not only a Kant but a Beethoven—not only a Darwin but a Carlyle. *Not in each of these, but in all, is human nature whole.* They are not opposed but supplementary—not mutually exclusive but reconcilable. And if, unsatisfied with them all, the human mind with the yearning of a pilgrim for his distant home, will still turn to the Mystery from which it has emerged, seeking to fashion it so as to give unity to thought and faith; so long as this is done, not only without intolerance or bigotry of any kind, but with the enlightened recognition that ultimate fixity of conception is here unattainable, and that each succeeding age must be held free to fashion the mystery in accordance with its own needs—then, casting aside all the restrictions of Materialism, I would affirm this to be a field for the noblest exercise of what, in contrast with the *knowing* faculties, may be called the *creative* faculties of man.[38]

If we accept the truth of this paragraph, and wish to see human nature whole; if we consider that it is part of the function of religion to pursue 'those unquenchable claims of man's moral and emotional nature which the understanding can never satisfy', then we Friends who have contributed so much to the achievements of science must turn to help redress the balance.

## 15

Let me end with my favourite character from Shakespeare, Nick Bottom the weaver. From his loom with its craftsman's dignity, where he is rich in self-esteem and the enthusiastic admiration of his fellows, he is drawn into the world of drama: the craftsman becomes an arts-man. In the process of rehearsal he has to leave the safety of daylight and the security of the city for the forest, the world of night and fantasy, untamed and untamable. He has dreamt of playing all the parts, including the heroine and the dreadful beast; but he has settled for the hero. And now, in the fairy-haunted forest, he is abandoned by his kind and becomes the sport of a disordered fairy kingdom. He is revealed as the ass he is; but even at the moment when they are all making an ass of him, and his donkey's head has become marvellous hairy about the face, he becomes aware of another dimension. Through the same magic which made an ass of him, he becomes the lover of the fairy queen. She may not share his tastes and she knows he is ridiculous, but she cannot help loving him. The enchantment works for the immortal as well as the mortal; she loves him as Venus loves the Lute-Player, for 'Eternity is in love with the products of Time'. So now Nick Bottom, who counted the threads of warp and weft, and knew how much an ell to charge for kersey,

> sees wonders of richness and delicacy never before known to such a simple, practical man: the profusion of swelling nature, apples, dewberries, purple grapes, green figs and mulberries; the microscopic elegancies of life, bags of honey-bees, tapers made of the waxen thighs of bees and 'lighted at the fiery glow-worm's eyes;' the unbelievably fine movements of the world beyond the literal eye. (So says Alvin Kernan, whose marvellous interpretation I have plundered for my purpose.)[39]

And then back to the city, where Nick Bottom and his friends will show us—at the Duke's wedding, no less—all the marvels of the imagination. Alas, their powers are not sufficient; they have chosen a tale of love, despair and death, but they are not quite up to it. But it doesn't pay to be superior; the spectators too are merely players in a play. They may laugh at Peter Quince and his troupe, but they had better watch out in case we laugh at *them* 'for taking their reality so seriously, and for closing off as mere dreams those further ranges of reality in the dark woods where they encountered the strange forces at work in themselves and their world'. They will go to bed at last, but the fairies will still be there.

Come, fellow Bottoms, fellow Hermias, Helenas and Lysanders, great Dukes and poor deaf Starvelings too; night has come, the moon is high, and the primrose banks shine in its light. It is time to go into the sacred wood, where strange and disconcerting experiences await us, where the briers will snatch at us and shadowy *doppelgängers* trap and confuse us, catching us in shaming postures of love and hate. But the dark powers will in the end stand our friends:

> And the country proverb known,
> That every man should take his own
> In your waking shall be shown:
> Jack shall have Jill,
> Nought shall go ill,
> The man shall have his mare again, and all shall be well.[40]

# REFERENCES AND NOTES

[1] Barclay (Robert) *Apology for the True Christian Divinity.* Prop. iii, 1678 London edn.

[2] Blake (William) 'Annotations to the Laocoon Group' in *Poetry and Prose of William Blake* ed. by Geoffrey Keynes. London: Nonesuch, 1932, rptd. 1961, p. 767

[3] Howitt (William) *The Yearbook of the Country*, December. London: Henry Colburn, N.D., pp. 401–3

[4] Barclay, *op. cit.*, p. 59. The quoted phrase on 'A masterpiece' is by the Belgian poet, Emile Verhaeren.

[5] Smart (Christopher) *Collected Poems* ed. by Norman Callan. Vol. 1 'Jubilate Agno'. London: Routledge, 1949, pp. 268, 313

[6] 'Mairzy Dotes', in MS. Sloane 4 (c. 1450) British Library. An early version of 'Scarborough Fair' is also dated early fifteenth century.

[7] Sewel (William) *History of the . . . Quakers*, 1669 edn., p. 487

[8] Eccles (Solomon) *A Musick-Lector*, 1667, pp. 12, 16

[9] For John Eccles see *New Oxford History of Music.* Vol 5, *Opera and Church Music 1630–1750* ed. by Anthony Lewis and Nigel Fortune, 1975, p. 28

[10] Fox (George) *Journal* ed. by J. L. Nickalls. London Yearly Meeting, 1952, rptd. 1975, p. 38

[11] Alton (Edwin H.) *Quakers and Music in the British Isles* (1965). Unpublished monograph in Friends House Library.

[12] Jones (William) *Quaker campaigns in Peace and War.* London: Headley Bros., 1899, p. 10

[13] *Report of the Manchester Conference, 1895.* London: Headley Bros., 1896, pp. 204–5

[14] *Samhain*, nos. 1–7, 1901–8 in one vol. ed. by W. B. Yeats. London: F. Cass, 1970, p. 190

[15] Roger-Marx (Claude) and Cotté (Sabine) *Delacroix*, trns. by Lynn Michelson. London: Pall Mall Press, 1970.

[16] 'De Profundis' in *Complete Works of Oscar Wilde* ed. Vyvyan Holland. London: Collins, rptd. 1969, p. 915

[17] Quoted as epigraph in *The Dyer's Hand* by W. H. Auden. London: Faber, 1963.

[18] *Christian Practice*, the second part of Christian Discipline. London Yearly Meeting, 1925, p. 76

[19] Horace, *Odes* IV, 9:25: Many brave men lived before Agamemnon, but eternal night lies on them all alike, unknown, unwept, for lack of a sacred poet.

[20] Dudbridge (Glen) *The Hsi-yu Chi: a study of antecedents to the sixteenth-century novel.* Cambridge University Press, 1970, p. 167
I express my acknowledgements to this fine book for the whole section on Wu Ch'eng-en's novels; and to William G. Sewell for much helpful advice.

[21] Wu Ch'eng-en *Monkey*, trns. by Arthur Waley. London: Allen & Unwin, 1942, rptd. 1953, pp. 266–7

71

[22] Yeats (W. B.) 'Emotions of Multitude' in *Ideas of Good and Evil*. 3rd edn., 1907, rptd. 1914, p. 237

[23] Nietzsche (F. W.) *The Birth of Tragedy* trns. by Francis Golffing. New York: Doubleday Anchor Books, 1956, pp. 136–7

[24] Artaud (Antonin) *The Theater and its Double* trns. by Mary Caroline Richards. New York: Grove Press, 1958, see 'The third letter', p. 116

[25] Castiglione (Baldassare) *The Courtier* trns. by Thomas Hoby. London: Dent Everyman's Library, rpt. 1937, p. 320

[26] Ceresole (Pierre) *Vivre sa Verité*. Neuchatel: à la Baconniere, 1950, p. 48. The statement was made in answer to a Sunday School teacher who (in essence) repeated Solomon Eccles's argument, that Satan seduces us through beauty. Ceresole, after the comment in the text, went on 'Cher ami, tu ne changeras pas ça. Tu t'es fait mépriser à travers les âges, à juste titre, pour avoir blasphémé.'

[27] Weil (Simone) *Waiting on God*. London: Collins Fontana, 1959, rptd. 1959, pp. 117–8, 120

[28] 'Letter to Richard Dehmel, 13 December 1912' in *Letters of Arnold Schoenberg* ed. by Erwin Stein. London: Faber, 1964, pp. 35–6

[29] Stedron (Bohimir) *Leos Janacek: letters and reminiscences*. Prague: Artis, 1955, p. 245

[30] Lawrence (D. H.) 'Benjamin Franklin' in *The Symbolic Meaning*. London: Centaur Press, 1962, pp. 38–9

[31] Quoted by Martin Esslin in *Theatre of the Absurd*. London: Eyre & Spottiswoode, 1961, p. 66, from *L'Aveu* by Arthur Adamov, 1938.

[32] Dennison (George) on Peter Schumann's play *Fire*, in *Tulane Drama View*, no. 47, 1966, pp. 36–7

[33] Auden (W. H.) 'Out on the lawn I lie in bed' in *Look Stranger*. London: Faber, 1935, p. 13 (One line altered in *Collected Shorter Poems*, p. 69)

[34] From 'Testimony of Francis Howgill concerning Edward Burrough' in Burrough's *Works* (1672) prelim leaf c 3.

[35] Snyder (Margaret) *A Man of Holy Simplicity:* tributes to the witness of Gurdial Mallik. Supplement to *The Friendly Way*. Kotagiri, South India, July 1970, p. 9

[36] Fox, *op. cit.*, pp. 232–3

[37] Translation of *The Iron Coin* by courtesy of the editor of *The Times Literary Supplement* in which it appeared (with the original Spanish by Jorge Luis Borges) on 6 August 1976.

[38] Tyndall (John) 'The Belfast Address' delivered before the British Association for the Advancement of Science on 19 August 1874; contained in his *Fragments of Science*, vol. 2, pp. 200–1

[39] Kernan (Alvin) '*Ducdame*, Shakespearean comedy to Twelfth Night' in *The Revels History of Drama in English*. London: Methuen, 1975, vol. 3, p. 316

[40] A Midsummer Night's Dream, Act III, Scene 2

For the section on Titian, I express my indebtedness to *The paintings of Titian* by Harold E. Wethey, vol. 3, Phaidon, 1975, and to the writings of Erwin Panofsky, especially *Problems in Titian, mostly Iconographic*, Phaidon, 1970.